THE CITY IN THE AMERICAN NOVEL,

1789-1900

THE CITY IN THE AMERICAN NOVEL,

1789-1900

A STUDY OF AMERICAN NOVELS PORTRAYING
CONTEMPORARY CONDITIONS IN NEW YORK,
PHILADELPHIA, AND BOSTON

GEORGE ARTHUR DUNLAP

NEW YORK / RUSSELL & RUSSELL

ACKNOWLEDGMENT

The subject for this dissertation was suggested to the writer by Dr. Arthur Hobson Quinn of the Department of English at the University of Pennsylvania. Throughout its preparation Dr. Quinn has been tireless in his words of counsel, encouragement, and constructive criticism. The writer is also indebted to Dr. Paul H. Musser of the same department for his discerning comments upon the completed manuscript. Librarians and their assistants were unfailingly courteous and helpful in obtaining the necessary books. The resources of the following libraries were used: The Library of the University of Pennsylvania; the Mercantile Library of Philadelphia; the Library Company of Philadelphia, the Free Library of Philadelphia; the New York Public Library, and the Library of Congress. At the latter institution the director of the Rare Book Room, Mr. V. Valta Parma, displayed a sincere, personal interest and was able to make important additions to the Bibliography, especially to that section dealing with city novels written before the Civil War.

G. A. D.

University of Pennsylvania, July 1, 1934.

CONTENTS

INTRODUCTION

The reader of the American novel may find it stimulating to examine systematically novels which represent contemporary life in our large cities. This should be particularly true of those novels that represent life in the cities chosen for study here. From the earliest days of our nation's history until the opening of the present century, these three cities—New York, Philadelphia and Boston—have reflected faithfully the changing conditions of American life as found in the populous centres. They represent, of course, only one section of the country—the eastern part—but they have received such careful and continuous attention from the novelists that they may be taken, collectively, to represent a homogeneous whole, the American city. It is true that other cities received notice from American authors, especially Chicago, New Orleans, San Francisco, and Washington. These, however, are newer cities and cannot illustrate urban life for the whole period under review as can the historic cities of New York, Philadelphia, and Boston. Furthermore, they lack geographical contiguity, and their citizens have not been so nearly homogeneous in their manners and customs as have been the citizes of the three cities selected.

The writer of this dissertation has a two-fold task: (1) to trace chronologically the facts about the various phases of life in the city which the contemporary novels record; and (2) to determine whether the same novels have qualities that make them of permanent literary value.

Before beginning a detailed review of these novels, it should be profitable to indicate briefly the growth of interest in the city on the part of our novelists. In very early novels such as *The Power of Sympathy* (1789) and others of a similar character, one may find scenes which are supposed to be urban, but they are so feebly identified that one may safely disregard them. Therefore, one must look to Hugh H. Brackenridge and his *Modern Chivalry* (1792) for the first definite indication of the city in our novel. After him, in the work of our first novelist of importance, Charles Brockden Brown, the reader may discover vivid representations of incidents occurring within the cities of Philadelphia and New York, as the author remembered them from his own experiences there. Then for a time sincere lovers of the city among American novelists were few. In the thirties one comes to Catherine Maria Sedgwick and Frederick W. Thomas. The former combined a fondness for the city with an equal fondness for the country. Thomas, though now virtually forgotten except for the fact that he was a warm friend of Edgar Allan Poe, deserves remembrance for his realistic glimpses into the city in *Clinton Bradshaw* (1835).

Fear of the city's alleged evils and wickedness and emphasis on its perils and miseries developed in the forties and fifties a type of story which foreshadowed the later dime novel both in its lurid qualities and in its popularity The efforts of several writers of this fiction will be included here, but for the most part attention will be directed to novels of higher artistic merit.

The 1860's saw the production of significant novels of the city by Bayard Taylor, George W. Curtis, and Theodore Winthrop. It is to be regretted that Taylor did not again return to the city as scene for his novels after writing *John Godfrey's Fortunes,* that Curtis did not continue in the regular novel after *Trumps,* and that Winthrop's work, so promising for the future, was suddenly stopped by his death in the inter-sectional conflict. Two other writers of this decade—Richard B. Kimball and Henry Morford—wrote novels that are instructive for the facts which they present of life in Northern cities during and shortly after the same war.

Mrs. Rebecca Harding Davis during the 1870's carried forward the realistic method of treating urban life that had already manifested itself in Brown's yellow fever episodes and Thomas's pictures of low life. Her scenes are surprisingly vivid when one reflects that she was not a complete convert to life in the city, judging from the unqualified praise of the rural scene now and then inserted into her works.

In the eighties and nineties the great increase in population of the cities was accompanied by a corresponding increase in the number of American novels describing life there. The problem for the historian was no longer, as in former decades, a problem of delving for material, but one of selection from a large mass of material. An idea of the popularity of the city in the fiction of the time may be gathered from a glance at the long list of novels of city life placed at the end of this work. There one may find more than one hundred authors, and of these, fifty-seven belong to the eighties and nineties. From this group those who were most successful in reproducing the life of the American city were the following: William Dean Howells, Henry C. Bunner, Henry Harland, S. Weir Mitchell, F. Marion Crawford, Charles Dudley Warner, Henry James Arlo Bates, Robert Grant, Paul Leicester Ford, Mrs. Ellen Olney Kirk, Edgar Fawcett, Edward Eggleston, Stephen Crane, Hamlin Garland, and Ellen Glasgow.

Selection of novels to form the basis of this study was made with the following principles in mind: (1) The novels must deal with contemporary life. (2) They must describe distinctive features of life in the city and not events that could have taken place anywhere else. (3) Characters in the novels must have been directly influenced by their residence within the city. (4) Novels may be rejected for consideration because of deficiency in literary merit, that is, because of pronounced weakness in character portrayal, or in style, or because they indulge in cheap sensationalism.

With the opening of the twentieth century came a still greater increase in the number of novels dealing with life in our American cities. There was also a marked change in method of writing and in topics treated. A new, more intense realism, already foreshadowed in the nineties, now came into full expression. Muckraking, or the exposure of corruption in municipal government, became popular with our novelists; and new social and industrial problems were discussed by them on a larger scale than formerly. On account of these developments and on account of the difficulties in obtaining the needed breadth of perspective with which to view novels of the present era, it was thought best to make the close of this treatise coincide with the close of the nineteenth century.

CHAPTER I

THE STRUGGLE FOR SUCCESS IN THE CITY

The struggle for success in a large city is a theme which offers great possibilities to the literary artist, especially one who uses such a broad medium as the novel. The adventurer may come from outside the city, or he may be city-born. In either case, his success or his failure is dependent very largely upon his own inherent nature. Clyde Fitch well expresses this truth in his tense drama, *The City,* when he has George Rand say: "What the City does is to bring out what's strongest in us. If at heart we're good, the good in us will win! If the bad is strongest, God help us! Don't blame the city! She gives the man his opportunity; it is up to him what he makes of' it!"

We may profitably consider what attractions the city offered to the newcomer. What induced him to journey there? Generally speaking, he came hoping to find there more favorable surroundings or enlarged opportunities. The farmer's boy, unwilling to till the soil as his father and perhaps his grandfather had done before him, believed that the city was the place where he could satisfy his passion for something new, something different. To him it was a place of escape. Many others, not reared on farms, found in it prospective havens of refuge from the unpleasant features of small-town life: its minimum of educational and cultural advantages and its maximum of interference in one's private affairs. One could lose oneself in the great city and begin life anew. One could remain secluded there indefinitely, if that was thought desirable, or one could make quick and numerous friendships, for good or bad. The newcomer may not have known these latter facts, but experience in the city soon taught them to him. For the future man of letters, the city offered invaluable association with others possessed of similar ambitions; it offered him periodicals and publishing houses where he might sell the product of his talents. For the painter and sculptor mention of the city suggested the art schools where he might perfect himself in his craft, and the studio life where he might practice his art in competition with his fellows. To the minister a call to the city church meant larger opportunities for service to mankind; to the lawyer and doctor, likewise, the city meant a challenge to greater efforts. The tradesman who had outgrown his village store dreamed of the city—its large commercial houses, department stores, perhaps Wall Street and an opportunity to make a fortune in the stock market. To the skilled workman the city offered larger factories and perhaps the chance to market a product of his own manufacture. To the reformer, or political aspirant, the city often was attractive as the seat of legislative bodies where he could voice his views on improvement of the existing order of things. And above all to the dishonest mind, the city was alluring as a centre where victims for his criminal practices could be obtained on the largest scale.

The native naturally does not look with as much awe upon the city as does the outsider. He accepts it as a matter of course, but at the same time, he seizes all the advantages which it provides with the air of one who is only claiming what is his own by right of possession. His adventures in his own environment do not invite the attention of the novelist as frequently as do the adventures of the newcomer to the city. To the superficial thinker, success in the city seems more of a surety to the native than to the outsider. As a matter of fact, both face the same stern competition and the same temptations of vice and crime. Will power, talent, and industry will assure the victory in the city struggle to either type of struggler, and lack of these qualifications will just as readily bring defeat.

In this first chapter we shall analyze, generally in chronological order, a number of instances of the struggle in the city, in a search for the reasons for success or failure, remembering that we are surveying the scene with the eyes of the contemporary.

The first illustration of any significance is the journey to Philadelphia of an unsophisticated country lad who leaves home on account of disapproval of his father's second marriage—to the milk-maid. This is Arthur Mervyn, a creation of our first professional man of letters, Charles Brockden Brown. Although critics have looked upon Arthur as just another representative of eighteenth-century fondness for the child of nature, we shall consider him here as a normal young man who has the normal adventures of a stranger in a large city. Like Benjamin Franklin, Arthur Mervyn found his entrance into Philadelphia attended with embarrassment. His was a too-trusting nature, as was to be expected from his rearing. Therefore, the reader sympathizes with his sour comment the next morning that the city is a place of "evil smells . . . and irksome companions." The suave Welbeck, worldly and criminal, notices the boy's innocent air as he looks enviously upon Quaker mansions with large gardens; and he has little difficulty in persuading him to reconsider his decision about going back home and to take employment as his copyist in one of those same fine homes (though not a Quaker's). Those first few days with Welbeck were trying ones, and the urge to abandon city ways came upon him again quite strongly. But before long, the appeal of the city has become so attractive that he can declare that "all the delights of sensation and refinements of intelligence" (perhaps we should now use the term "culture") were to be found there, and would be nearly wanting altogether in the country. It is not surprising, therefore, that he stays with his patron until the latter mysteriously disappears beneath the waves of the peaceful Delaware.

On a second visit Arthur meets with some trying experiences in connection with the plague, and his adventures with the enraged Welbeck and with the charming Clemenza Lodi whom he rescues from a home in a disreputable quarter of the city. But he is no longer a rustic; the city has converted him into one of its devotees. There he has met men who inspire him with respect and love; and he affirms that "if cities are the chosen seats of misery and vice, they are likewise the soil of all the laudable and strenuous productions of mind."*

Arthur's ambitions for city usefulness lie in the direction of medicine, owing, no doubt, to association with Dr. Stevens who nursed him through the yellow fever. Unfortunately, the author does not inform us of the outcome of his studies, though we do read that he was allowed to accompany the doctor on professional

---

*Brown, Charles Brockden—"Arthur Mervyn", 2 vols., Phila., 1799-1800. Reference is to edition of 1857, vol. 2, p. 73.

visits. We learn too that the young man gains a certainty of his own importance and that he hopes some day "to lay claim to the gratitude and homage" of his fellow men. But he becomes intrigued with thoughts of a social existence, and it is with adventures of a social nature that the remainder of the novel is concerned. We should like, for the sake of completeness, to learn whether he became a successful physician, and if he still continued to prefer the city to the country environment. Denied answer to these questions, we cannot, of course, state positively whether Arthur Mervyn won a final success or failure in the city.

Clinton Bradshaw, in a novel by Frederick W. Thomas,† is another farmer boy who strives for success in a large city, presumably New York. He is a law student and distinguished among his fellows for skill in their debating society which meets to discuss such serious problems as "Whether woman was equal to man in intellect." Like his companions, he was fond of spending pleasant hours at one of the city's many oyster saloons, but afterwards in his own room, no matter how late the hour, he would glance over the life of Caesar, Themistocles, Napoleon or Chatham, or study a chapter on executory devises, and then read from a fashionable novel before going to sleep. A young man endowed with such powers of endurance, and in addition, equipped with the natural gifts of an orator was certain of success.

Like Arthur Mervyn, Bradshaw did not fear to explore the unsavory sections of the city, and like him also, he aided in the rescue of an innocent young woman imprisoned there. His law practice, indeed, was largely built upon his wide acquaintance with criminals whom he did not hesitate to accept as clients. The interest of the novel is not so much in the plot as in its portrayal of certain features of the life in a large American city. These include revelations of law-student life; Bradshaw's unique method of qualifying for criminal practice by taking his examiner into an oyster saloon and making him a glass of whiskey punch; the scenes at night in the city's dark streets and alleys; the description of gangs of toughs, and of the activities of the all-important watchmen, one of whom is depicted as an out-and-out bully; and

---

†Thomas, Frederick W.—"Clinton Bradshaw", 2 vols., Phila., 1835.

the court-room scene where Bradshaw proves the prosecuting attorney to be a grafter. In the end, Bradshaw has risen to be a leading attorney and has been victorious in a contest for representative in Congress despite charges of scandal brought against him. He has marched steadily forward without a set-back. We never have doubted his ultimate success from the start. In this respect the story of his struggles for recognition in the city may be said to be weak, but it is a fault common to the American fiction of the thirties. An article in the *Southern Literary Messenger** objects to the novel on other grounds: (1) for its introduction of characters from the low life of the city, a practice declared to be out of fashion; and (2) because the characters were such every-day people who lacked the saving grace of magic and romance, which in the critic's opinion have been since the days of Mrs. Radcliffe necessary ingredients of the successful American novel. But what to this critic seemed objectionable qualities in the novel are now generally accepted as praiseworthy qualities, for they enable the reader to obtain there truthful pictures of an American city of the thirties, which he could not obtain, for example, from Theodore S. Fay's *Norman Leslie*,† written in the same year.

The American city continued to provide copy for our novelists. Writers of sensational fiction delighted in depicting the miseries of existence there; and those who wrote more conservatively and with more attention to style and character portrayal, found inspiration in a city which was constantly changing to meet the requirements of the growing industrialism. By 1850 there was at least one novelist finding inspiration in the Industrial Revolution as it affected the cities. This was Sylvester Judd, whose *Richard Edney* (1850) describes the experiences of a young mechanical expert in a mythical city of the author's invention called Woodylin. Edney comes there fresh from the village and lacking any semblance of respect for city ways. On the very first day he lectures

---

*vol. 4, pp. 296-301 (May, 1838).

†This novel was unmercifully ridiculed by Edgar Allan Poe, but *Clinton Bradshaw* received his approbation for its "frank, unscrupulous portraiture of men and things, in high life and low", and its "unusual discrimination and observation in respect to character." (See "The Works of Edgar Allan Poe", 10 vols., Chicago, 1896, vol. 9, 214-5.)

his fellow workmen in the saw-mill upon the evils of intemperance, and breaks the bottles of a liquor-peddler who gains an entrance there. He is perfect in habits, strong physically and even more a child of nature than Arthur Mervyn. The author uses him merely as a mouth-piece for the expression of his theories for the curing of the evils which flourish in the city. Therefore, he is not a proper illustration of the success-or-failure theme, for he cannot possibly fail. Evidently he has never made a mistake in his life. In short, he is not a real person. The novel itself evidences understanding of urban conditions of the times, but the author exercised poor judgment in couching his ideas not in the usual fictional form, but rather in the style of an elaborate, though unattractive, essay.

Thus far the illustration of the struggle for success has come from the main characters and has received the predominant attention of the authors. But in *Married or Single* by Miss Sedgwick (1857) this struggle is a subordinate element, the main theme being that of woman's right to an independent career. The adventurer is another young attorney—Archibald Lisle—who, at his initial appearance in social circles still has vestiges of the rustic clinging to him. In his awkwardness he spills a wine glass over the silk dress of his companion, thus gaining the contempt of the city-bred, supercilious Copley. But as an advocate before the bar of justice Lisle soon shows that he has few equals among the younger men of the profession. Moreover, he is virtuous and gallant, while Copley is dissipated and immoral. Lisle's labors at the law injure his health, because, as Miss Sedgwick carefully explains, he reserved no intervals for recreation or social refreshment; consequently, a trip abroad is suggested. Unlike most of Theodore Fay's heroes, who seem to divide their time between United States and Europe, Lisle is quickly brought home again to face the problem of securing a wife. This proves much more troublesome to him than his legal struggles, for several young women whom he knew in Mapleton have come as strangers to the big city and now look to him for advice and protection. One of them meets her death in a lodging-house fire (such fires are common in city novels of this time); another, Alice Clifford, comes asking assistance for her brother, jailed for forgery. A court-room scene follows, and, as we should expect, Lisle's skillful defence proves the defendant absolutely guiltless. City sharpers had taken advantage of his rural inexperience. Lisle proposes to Alice, mistaking her gratitude for love, but is chagrined to discover that she is already betrothed to another. The scene of the story shifts to the country, which to Miss Sedgwick, is just as attractive, if not more so, than the city. Lisle's efforts towards matrimony are crowned with final joy when he obtains the young woman he had admired from the first, the very one who had dreamed splendid visions of the excellent opportunities open to a single woman, but who now yields to the "happier fate" which she decides is reserved for her as wife of a brilliant metropolitan lawyer.

Lisle's experiences, as far as they are related in the novel, are not useful as examples of a struggle for success. The opposition to his triumph was too trivial, consisting as it did merely of a crudity in manners which he overcame without difficulty. His talents soon brought the city at his feet, but things rarely happened that way in real life, even in the fifties. The novel is an improvement in many ways over the work of Thomas and Judd, though the male characters are generally inferior in strength and reality to the female characters. Lisle himself risks disapproval by his indecisiveness in love matters, a characteristic which is in marked contrast with his invariable success in his law cases.

In *John Godfrey's Fortunes* (1865) city forces wage a sterner battle against one, who because he is a strange mixture of strong and weak elements, is far from being a model hero. Bayard Taylor, the author, takes Godfrey through many characteristic scenes of rural and small-town life before bringing him into the city. As equipment for a New York career, he can count upon a well-grounded education and skill at verse writing. He had already experienced a love affair, had quarreled with his uncle over religious matters and had taught in a country school. In the city he becomes a hack writer and also brings out a book of poems which is favorably received. Promotion to a reporter's post in the city department of a local newspaper brings him $15 a week and permits him to move from his first cheap boarding-house at Mrs. Very's to a more genteel one on Bleecker Street, west of Broadway. The group whom he finds there are not, however, more pleasing to his taste; indeed, the young idealistic Swansford, musician and composer, whom he met at Mrs. Very's, continues to be his warmest friend.

The chief impediments to Godfrey's continued progress in the city are of two kinds: first, his unfortunate association with Brandagee, a literary light who establishes a new periodical, *The Oracle,* and engages him to write smartly cynical stories and articles for it; and, second, his kind-heartedness which leads him to assist the unfortunate Jane Berry to escape from a disorderly house during the confusion consequent upon a fire in a house nearby. In this action, despite his expressed wish not to play the part of hero, he invites association with Arthur Mervyn, Clinton Bradshaw and Archibald Lisle, all of whom gave timely assistance to "females" in distress. Godfrey manages to secure a pleasant home for Jane who, he learns, is a country girl lured into a wrong environment through ignorance; rumors that she is his mistress cause him to lose for a time the friendship of the young heiress whom he expected to marry. This disappointment, in turn, causes him to lose control over himself, and it is not long before Brandagee and his Bohemian friends have dragged him into gambling and drinking habits. His writing standards deteriorate until he is satisfied with turning out cheap sensationalism and even accepts a commission to write advertisements in the form of verse for a new dentifrice. In a comment upon his own degradation, Godfrey writes: "Once the imagined brother of Irving, Bryant, and Longfellow, I now found myself the rival of Napoleon B. Quigg and Julia Cary Reinhardt! I had reached indeed the lowest pit of literature."* His moral recovery comes about through a boyhood chum, Bob Simmons, who revives his lost self-respect and persuades him to leave his worthless associates. The latter part of the novel is disappointing, for it does not give any further extended account of his literary adventures, but instead shows his ultimate triumph to be the outcome of winning the hand of the young heiress whom he had long been wooing. He, too, becomes the recipient of a modest sum, so that between

---

*Taylor, Bayard, "John Godfrey's Fortunes," New York, 1865, 429.

them they have $100,000 with which to face the future. Godfrey's novel, for most literary adventurers in the city write novels, is his autobiography. In other words, it is *John Godfrey's Fortunes*. He is an example of the young man who wins out in the city but only after a severe struggle, in which his strength of character aids him, as does also the providential appearance of a friend of steadier habits than his who saves him from moral and physical ruin.

While Godfrey surrendered some of his literary ideals by turning from the writing of verse to the more lucrative journalism, his friend Swansford remained loyal to his high aspirations until the end. And that end was tragic, for, over-worked by the writing of a classical symphony be became seriously ill and died. Swansford's martyrdom to his art was wholly unnecessary, for relatives and friends in his native Connecticut town had long been anxious to have him return to them, but like many others gifted with artistic talents, he would not give up his struggle and preferred to fight on.

The difficulties facing the aspirant for a secure place in the urban world are further emphasized in the novels of Richard B. Kimball, a New Englander, who practiced law in New York city from 1840 to 1854, then transferred his activities to literature and became a valued contributor to the *Knickerbocker Magazine* and *Putnam's*. Kimball's philosophy in regard to the city was an orthodox one, but unfortunately he lacked the ability to write an entertaining story. His novels, therefore, have mostly been forgotten but deserve attention for the information they reveal of contemporary business conditions in our metropolis during the fifties and sixties.

The first of Kimball's four novels of New York life, *Revelations of Wall Street* (*Knickerbocker,* 1861-1862) is open to criticism for use of technical business terms without sufficient explanation to make them intelligible to the general reader. Here is presented the autobiography of Charles E. Parkinson, a New Yorker, who has failed in the wholesale grocery business and attempts a recovery at the age of fifty by entering into Wall Street as a note-broker. His business ventures are described with tiresome detail. A domestic interest provided by the loyalty of his daughter is not sufficient to offset the monotony of the business chapters relating Parkinson's succession of losses.   At the climax, during the national crisis of August, 1857, when he is behind in office and house rent and cannot borrow even a five dollar bill, he receives a letter that solves all his troubles.   It announces the gift of $30,000 left to him through the will of a college classmate. Everything thus ends happily.   The novel does not come up to the expectations suggested by its title, for, while the revelations of Wall Street life are no doubt accurate, they are not particularly interesting owing to the fact that they were written not from the viewpoint of the large financier but from that of the small operator or note-broker.

In the second of these novels, *Was He Successful?* (1864) there is an early appearance in fiction of the city millionaire who after amassing a fortune finds himself still unhappy.   The moralistic intention of the author is seen in the query of the title.   The answer, as suggested by the thread of the story, is emphatically in the negative.   Hiram Meeker had conquered in city trade after a careful preliminary study of the mercantile methods of the small towns.   He had made his fortune and had married a rich girl belonging to one of New York's aristocratic families, but all these circumstances had not taught him the fact that real happiness in life, especially in the city, comes only to those who have taken an active interest in the lives of their less fortunate citizens. A paralytic stroke causes Meeker to realize his mistake more keenly.   He thus becomes significant in our fiction as a forerunner of numerous business men in our large cities who disregard the warnings of impending physical collapse until too late. Meeker had not only failed to participate in philanthropies but had also neglected to take proper supervision of the lives of his children so that it is not surprising that his unhappiness is further increased by various indiscretions on their part.

Henry Powers (Banker), 1868, is a great improvement, for the moral element is not over-stressed, the sections dealing with business life are made more readable, and the characters are, on the whole, more attractive.   The hero is a young man who, like Meeker, migrated to New York from New England.   The resemblance stops there, for Powers' personality was a pleasing one from the first, whereas Meeker's was always repelling. Powers made a phenomenal rise in a few years, but this was cut short by the Civil War which brought ruin to the commercial house that had already promised him a junior partnership. After serving with the Union army and receiving a severe wound which led to an honorable discharge, but from which he recovered, Powers returned to New York. The elderly man with whom he became associated there—Horace Deems—used methods closely resembling those of the exploiter. Through his own personal efforts, Powers was able to convert one of Deems' fraudulent schemes into an honest one that for a time benefited many of New York's poorer citizens by supplying them with coal at cost price. Eventually, of course, the upright Powers withdraws from his connection with Deems and does it without besmirching his own good name. Thenceforth, he begins to earn the reputation of being a young man who bids fair to make a mark for himself in the financial world. This he does when he and his partner take advantage of the gold situation in the spring of 1864 and clear nearly $250,000 each.

Henry Powers fought against Wall Street as did Parkinson but was younger and his struggle came when the financial world was not in so precarious a situation as it was when Parkinson had his trials. The younger man was optimistic in his judgment of the Street; he declared that except for a small class of human spiders —generally old men (among whom we may well include Meeker) —the vice of avarice is not fostered or encouraged. But to any one entering the Street as combatant he offers this advice: "Make yourself hard. Keep yourself entirely under martial law."*

The fourth of Kimball's New York novels, *To-Day (Putnam's Magazine,* 1869) relates the fortunes not of a single individual but of a group of individuals who come to the city. It adds little to his theory of life as it has been gleaned from the other works. Briefly stated, this theory teaches that the city generally crowns with success those who enter it equipped with adequate talent, honest ambition, and steadfast purposes, and condemns to failure those who permit their careers to be ruled by extravagance, greed,

---

*Kimball, Richard B.—"Henry Powers (Banker) How He Achieved a Fortune and Married," New York, 1868, 334.

dishonesty, or immorality. Kimball is persistent in showing that the desirable goal for which to strive in the city is not material possessions alone, but a combination of the material and spiritual. Happiness in the city, he believes, comes only to those who are willing to share a part of their advantages with those less fortunate than themselves. He was sincere in his efforts to depict the contemporary life of the city and some of its problems, but his range was restricted mostly to business conditions, and his novelistic touch was not the sure touch of a skilled craftsman. William Dean Howells, writing only a few years later, was able to provide a much broader range for the city novel and an infinitely superior technique. His solutions of urban problems are more intricate than Kimball's or those of the predecessors of Kimball. With Howells, honest ambition does not always bring success, nor do greed, dishonesty, and kindred vices always bring failure.

Six of Howells' novels may be selected for a study of his use of the success-or-failure motive. The first, in order of chronology, is *A Modern Instance* (1882). Bartley Hubbard, the principal character in this story, comes to Boston with his bride, Marcia, the daughter of a small-town attorney in whose office Hubbard had studied law in his spare moments, while editing the "Equity City Press." He was not unfamiliar with Boston, for while at college he had visited at the home of a Boston classmate, Ben Halleck. At that time he had quickly learned the city manners and dress, and there seemed to him little doubt of success when he came there to earn his living. His attractive personality was in his favor, though a too obvious selfishness tended to react against him. His failure in the large city environment is not easily explained. It is characteristic of Howells' fiction that he made his characters so evenly balanced with good and evil qualities that very little was needed to turn the scale one way or the other. Hubbard's fascination with journalism as he found it in Boston and the ease with which he made money by his writing drove from his mind all his former firm resolves to complete the study of law. This was unfortunate, for the greater seriousness of purpose which legal study would have induced in him, would have tended to deter him from that over-indulgence in the vices of drinking and gambling and from those violations of newspaper ethics that led directly to loss of his position and indirectly to all his later difficulties. His wife, too, contributed to his downfall by her inability to adapt herself to the city, and by her aversion to those features of its life which most attracted her husband, namely: attendance at concerts, lectures, and theatres. And it was one of her frequent fits of jealousy that caused Hubbard's desertion of her at a time when he had resolved upon complete reformation of his habits. In the final analysis, however, his failure was the result of his own deficiencies. The greater opportunities of city life did not with him, as with others, serve as welcome outlets for talents formerly imprisoned within the narrow limits of the small town, but seemed to draw out the roots of an unprincipled nature which might never have been revealed in the other environment. Howells shows clearly in this novel by his keen analysis of the character of Bartley Hubbard that he believed that the city will bring out the best or worst in a man. More specifically, he believed that if an individual who comes to the city has any inherent serious flaw in his character, the city will surely increase it. Since Howells always insisted upon carrying his characters mercilessly to the destination towards which they were drifting, the outcome for a person like Hubbard could not have been otherwise than tragic.

The struggles of Helen Harkness (*A Woman's Reason*, 1883) in the same city do not arouse as much suspense as to the final outcome as do those of Bartley Hubbard. The reader understands that Howells is using her as an illustration of the helplessness of the average woman of the city in the seventies to earn her own living. The reader also realizes that Helen may receive aid at any time that she wishes to ask for it, from former friends of the social world. Pride keeps her from this, except for one occasion when illness forces her to accept the hospitality of Clara Kingsbury. Her final deliverance from the city comes not as a result of her own efforts but through the opportune return of her supposedly drowned lover. By her acceptance of his offer of marriage all necessity for fighting against the stubborn, unsympathetic business world is removed. During her struggle her experiences presented an apt illustration of Howells' belief that the city was a stern taskmaster for a young woman of fashion who, like Helen, was without practical training. Her education had caused her to become enthusiastic in turn over French, music, and German, but, as the author satirically comments, she was after all, "merely and entirely a lady, the most charming thing in the world and, as regards anything but a lady's destiny the most helpless."* When her father's sudden death left her with only $5,000 she bravely but injudiciously resolved to be independent of all assistance. Her attempts to earn money are ridiculously futile owing to her general deficiency in talent, and her visits to Boston art and curio shops, loaded down with decorated pottery provide the best scenes of the novel. Howells is clever in his subtle exposition of Helen's very strong reluctance to let it be known that her vases are for sale. At the first shop when her work is highly complimented, she cannot bolster up courage enough to disillusion them of their impression that she has come there merly to exhibit it, and therefore leaves without endeavoring to make a sale. Similarly, at her boarding-house when Cornelia Root, the artist, sees the pottery, Helen quickly states that she had decorated it for a wedding present. At the dinner table she explains her day's activities by saying that she has been shopping. She does not describe the nature of her shopping—that, as it seemed to her, she was "the only one of all her sex who wished to sell and not to buy."† Hers is not an unusual situation in urban life. Loss of money frequently brings about such pathetic scenes as Howells has painted. The novel is significant for the author's discriminating study of the feminine mind as found in Helen Harkness, and for the demonstration of his ability to arouse the reader's sympathy for her without the use of pathos or sentiment.

In *A Modern Instance* Howells pictured a young man from a small town coming to grief in the large city. In his masterpiece, *The Rise of Silas Lapham* (1885) he shows an older man meeting defeat there and being forced to return to his native Vermont hills. Lapham is a more engaging person than Hubbard despite the series of blunders which he commits. A fortune had been made by him through his paint business, but this gradually disappears as a result of stock speculations and ill-advised loans to

---

*Howells, William Dean—"A Woman's Reason", New York, 1883, 137.
†ibid., p. 186.

business acquaintances. He could have recovered everything if he had been willing to become a party to a transaction which, to all outward appearances, is honest enough, but which he knows will ultimately victimize innocent buyers. The temptation is great but Lapham's natural integrity will not allow him to commit the fraud. Bankruptcy is the inevitable result. On the social side, Lapham finds city forces again allied against him. By birth and education he and his wife are essentially not on a par with the Back Bay set to which they aspire. In a way, Lapham realizes this, but his wife and daughters persuade him to build a house in a more fashionable part of Boston. His relations with the Coreys, who are of the socially élite, are friendly, but there is a wide gulf between them that even Penelope's marriage to Tom Corey cannot bridge. The burning of the new home before it is completed is a great financial blow but a blessing in disguise, for it hastens Lapham's removal from an environment in which he could never have been entirely happy. He comes out of all his difficulties with clean hands. Though he had failed in his struggle with the city, his failure was not the result of weakness, but is best explained by the assertion that he was out of his element there. A certain amount of rurality clung to him which continuous exposure to the city could not seem to eradicate. As Sewell, the minister, declared after a visit to him, the Colonel (Lapham) was more of a colonel in the Vermont hills than he had ever been on the Back Bay. Lapham is a great character creation. Though all his faults are ruthlessly exposed by the author, the reader retains a keen affection for him, owing to the sympathetic way in which he is drawn. The novel itself is a realistic study of the city's apparent triumph over a person who is not by nature equipped to withstand some of its sterner features. Howells raises the story above the commonplace by the fact that though he allows his hero to succumb in a material way to the city in the loss of his business interests, at the same time he shows him rising spiritually to new heights, so that his retirement to the country at the conclusion is very much in the nature of a victory.*

---

*Discussion of the city adventures of Lemuel Barker in *The Minister's Charge*, 1887, which would come at this point chronologically, has been reserved for the chapter on The Religious Life of the City.

In *A Hazard of New Fortunes* (1890) Howells has grouped together the experiences of a number of individuals who are newcomers to New York city. He is working in this novel upon a broad canvas, as is evident when he notes the fierce struggle for existence and declares, using Basil March as spokesman: "The whole at moments seemed to him lawless, godless; the absence of intelligent, comprehensive purpose . . ."*

Into this turmoil comes March and his wife direct from Boston where he had been engaged in the insurance business. Now he was about to try the larger, more difficult battlefield of New York. He had been called there by a literary promoter, Fulkerson, to become editor of the latter's new project, the *Every Other Week*. The change from one city to another did not affect him greatly. It was in one respect a welcome change, for he rejoiced to find in New York a splendid field for the writing of local-color sketches. Mrs. March was more disturbed, for New York to her seemed big, hideous and frantic; she complained that the people forgot even death there.

Another newcomer to New York was Dryfoos, the millionaire backer of the new journal. He was a Pennsylvania German who had made a fortune in natural gas and real estate, and came to the city as Fulkerson said, "to spend his money and get his daughters into the old Knickerbocker society." With him, the intellectual March found it hard to maintain congenial relations, because their interests were so widely separated. March's ambitions were centered about *Every Other Week,* but to Dryfoos the magazine was a minor matter; he was reported to have read only one of its articles in its first year of existence. Its profit of $25,000 seemed to him trivial. Contemptuously, he boasted that he had made that much in half a day in his own town in western Pennsylvania and had seen it made in half a minute sometimes in Wall Street. His indifference to the magazine's affairs suddenly ceased when at a staff dinner, Lindau, a foreign translator, expressed violent disagreement with his capitalistic views. The next morning he demanded of March that Lindau be dismissed. March

---

*Howells, William Dean—"A Hazard of New Fortunes", 2 vols., New York, 1890, vol. 1, 244.

refused on the ground that the objection to the man was in regard to his personal opinions and had nothing to do with his work for the magazine. March was angered at what he considered interference with the paper's management, since he regarded Fulkerson as the only one from whom he had to receive orders. The matter was settled by Lindau himself when he decided that he could not take money from an enterprise supported by a capitalist like Dryfoos. For a few hours, however, March and his wife and children were grieved to think that they would be forced to leave New York and probably return to Boston. This would have been a keen disappointment, for now that they had become accustomed to the metropolis, life in Boston would have been very distasteful. It no longer would have seemed like home to them. They had grown to like the touch-and-go quality of New York life and found it a pleasing contrast to the intense identification of Boston life; they liked the foreign quality of New York, "the flavor of olives, which, once tasted, can never be forgotten"; they enjoyed sitting "in the softening evenings among the infants and dotards of Latin extraction in Washington Square, safe from all who ever knew them"; March himself liked to stroll through the quaintness of Greenwich Village on a Sunday when his wife's "hereditary Sabbatarianism" kept her at home. No doubt a great deal of this attraction of New York to them was that the foreign faces and vestures seen there reminded them of similar faces and vestures that they had beheld a few years before in their European travels. The settlement of the dispute with Dryfoos and the assurance that they would remain in New York were therefore very gratifying to them. March turned his enthusiasm for the city into a series of articles on various features of its life; these were greatly admired when published.

The plot, as usual with Howells, was not the important thing. In the struggle with city life, Basil March was, of course, successful; and Dryfoos failed. His great wealth could not change his character, nor could it teach him that he was at fault in his treatment of his noble-hearted, charitably-inclined son whose nature was so different from his own. The sudden death of the son and soon afterwards the death of Lindau sobered him considerably. At the end of the story he and his wife and two daughters have gone to Europe and there have gained the social success denied to them in New York.

This novel does not offer so clear-cut a presentation of the success-or-failure theme as some of the other novels of Howells already considered. Its special significance is that it presents more detailed and more vivid side-lights of life in New York city than do any of his other works. He is here paying his respects to the city to which he himself had removed recently to do editorial work for *Harper's*.*

New York city again provides the setting for a struggle in *The World of Chance* (1893). Here we find an amplification of the theory expressed in *A Hazard of New Fortunes* that this is an "economic chance-world." Chance, as represented by a series of fortunate accidental circumstances, ensures the success of Shelley Ray in the New York literary world. He had come to that city from Midland in a rural section of New England, bringing with him the manuscript of a psychological novel dealing with hypnotism and entitled *A Modern Romeo*. The title was a fortunate selection since it suggested to Mr. Brandreth to whom Ray submitted the book, pleasant memories of an amateur performance of *Romeo and Juliet* in which he had a part. An intimacy was thus started which proved peculiarly valuable to Ray, for though Brandreth's manuscript readers reject the novel, he himself remains favorable to it and decides to publish it. Another work was being considered for acceptance by the firm at the same time, but on the day set aside for its perusal, Brandreth and his wife found themselves so worn out after a night of listening to their baby's series of crying spells that they did not feel equal to the task. Hence they interpreted this as a sign to bring out *A Modern Romeo* which they had already read. Chance further played a part in the success of the novel at a time when its sale was very tardy. The flattering review in the *Metropolis* which caused a decided reaction in its favor was not written by the regular critic of that journal but by a substitute who took the book home by mistake and was attracted to it because he had just been reading treatises on hypnotism. After Ray had achieved

---

*Angus Beaton, the well-drawn artist of this novel, will receive consideration in the chapter on the Literary and Artistic Life of the City.

recognition as one of New York's promising young novelists, he stopped to analyze his good fortune, and noted with chagrin all the accidental circumstances connected with it. But deep reflection caused him to reach this comforting conclusion: "Nothing . . . that seemed chance was really chance. It was the operation of a law so large that we caught a glimpse of its vast orbit once or twice in a life time. It was Providence."* Thus, it would seem that Howells at the close of the novel felt that perhaps he had been guilty of carrying his philosophy of chance a little too far, and must therefore make retraction in an identification of Chance with a divine purpose. Also it should be remembered that he was writing primarily about only one phase of city life: the entrance into literature and the obstacles thereto, the details of which were perfectly well known to him from personal observation. And we must allow for a large proportion of good-humored satire in his implication that success in literature is dependent entirely upon chance. Certainly, the reader should not carry the philosophy so far as to make it refer to success or failure in all phases of a city's life.†

The device used in *The Minister's Charge* of developing the character of a young rustic by showing him in contact with an older man who is well-versed in the ways of the city is cleverly employed again by Howells in *The Landlord at Lion's Head* (1897), another of his great novels. Here, the older man is Westover, an accomplished artist and a personage of social prominence in the city; and his younger acquaintance is the genial but uncouth Jeff Durgin with whom he has become well acquainted in visits to the summer mountain hotel owned by Jeff's mother. Westover is not responsible for Jeff's appearance in the city, but he feels a friendly interest in the young "jay"; and the latter consults him often when he gets into trouble in Boston or at Harvard, where his mother has sent him to prepare for the law. The artist's sound advice on these occasions is always given in a kindly manner, for he finds it difficult to get angry with Jeff no

---

*Howells, William D.—"The World of Chance," New York, 1893, 375.

†Denton's city adventures as described in "The World of Chance" will be considered in the chapter dealing with The Religious Life of the City, for his acts are governed largely by religious impulses.

matter how perplexed he may be at the continuance of his unconventional, and often offensive, actions. Jeff is grateful for Westover's interest in him, but seems totally unable to check an element of cruelty and thoughtlessness in his nature which crops out at uncertain intervals. His misdeeds may ultimately be traced to boredom with the city, for he was there only under protest and felt that his real post was at the hotel, where he could train himself to become the next landlord. Jeff is admirably sketched and is a real creation, even though we do not approve of his actions. The story's solution has no connection with the city but comes through the deaths of Jeff's elder brother and his mother, when he becomes owner and landlord of the inn, thus attaining his long-desired wish. It cannot be stated flatly that Jeff Durgin was ill-adapted to survive in the city. Far from it. But it can be stated that under the conditions in which he was living there in his college days he was certain to become a social misfit. He was discontented and not interested in his classes, and being strong of body and stubborn of mind, he naturally sought an outlet for his ill nature and obtained it in various ways that could not but earn the disapproval of the social world. In this sense, then, he was a failure in the city; but under different circumstances, as, for example, after his marriage with the worldly Genevieve Vostrand, we can well imagine that he could spend many satisfactory winters in Boston or any other large city. Uncouth and untrustworthy he would probably always remain, yet there are in the most cultured of our cities many others of the same calibre with whom he could be thoroughly congenial. Jeff Durgin, therefore, seems neither peculiarly rural nor urban, but cosmopolitan, for men of his type may, unfortunately, be found anywhere.

Judging from the evidence presented by the principal characters in the novels here studied, it would seem that Howells believed that the newcomer to the city fails more often than he succeeds. The only complete successes are those of Shelley Ray and Basil March. Of course, Silas Lapham gained a great deal in strength of character by his years of sojourn there; but the fact remains that after his misfortunes he returned to what seemed a more congenial native environment. The others were unqualified failures. We have seen that Bartley Hubbard's character was ruined in the city, that Helen Harkness failed in her efforts to earn her own living there, and that Jeff Durgin was out of sympathy with the city during his stay there, and it would have been much better for him if he had remained away from it and had been permitted to engage in some active occupation such as the management of his mother's hotel.

Grandison Mather (1889), written by Henry Harland four years before *The World of Chance,* treats a similar theme of literary adventures. Like Howells, Harland was concerned with problems of the New York publishing world, but his emphasis was upon a different phase of that world than Howells'. He showed that success there for the writer of fiction is greatly simplified if he is able to get his novel into the hands of a publisher who specializes in that particular type of fiction to which it belongs. Thus, the first one to whom Tom Gardiner's *Dreams Within a Dream* was submitted, rejected it on the grounds of crudity. Everett St. Marc, a competent critic, explained this to Tom by declaring that the publisher though a cultured man was mortally afraid of the crude and unconventional. The second one accepted the book because he liked the unconventional.

Success came from the joint efforts of man and wife, for it was Tom's talented wife who finished his second effort, a Christmas novel, when he himself had suffered a break-down and the novel was over-due. This is a rather improbable touch, for Mrs. Gardiner was not at all experienced in writing. She further helps out by the steady income from her position as soloist in a church choir.

The belief that an author does not usually succeed in New York's literary world through acceptance of one book alone is presented here, when it is shown that Gardiner's scanty royalties from his first novel begin to increase appreciably when his second one makes its appearance. Harland's novel is significant for its brilliant sketches of Bohemianism in a New York boarding-house. All who dwell there are striving for success in the city. One is an author and lecturer on religious topics; another is a singing-master; a third is a pianist and teacher; a fourth is a private secretary. All are congenial despite differences of nationality and creed.

In strong contrast with both Harland's and Howells' treatments of the novelist in the large city is that of F. Marion Crawford in *The Three Fates* (1892). Here the emphasis is laid upon the genius of the author and not upon the methods or chance of getting his work before the public. George Wood, the hero, enters novel-writing through the gate-way of the book review and similar hack-work. He is himself without financial resources, but by virtue of his mother's social position in the city he is received without question into its richest homes. In this manner he meets his "three fates." By the earnest entreaties of one of them, Constance Fearing, he is persuaded to begin his first creative work, the chapters of which, one by one, he reads to her as they sit together on a Central Park bench. In twenty-four days it is finished; and his enthusiastic critic, not sharing his disdain for it, takes it and succeeds in securing a publisher for it. Thus, placement, which was so difficult a problem for Shelley Ray and Tom Gardiner, proves to be easy for the resourceful Constance; but Crawford was probably more intent upon developing the character of his hero than he was with details of literary acceptance or rejection.

Although Wood becomes a celebrated novelist, he is shown to be little different from his companions in ordinary affairs of life. Indeed, he is notoriously indecisive, especially in love affairs. In his periods of inspiration, however, he more than fulfills the requirements of true genius. His actions then are, of course, somewhat idealized, to make them conform with the conception that most people have of the working methods of a great writer. Thus, when he is writing, nothing can arouse him, not even the news of his inheritance of a great fortune. Unlike most seekers after success in the city, Wood cares very little for money. What he wishes for particularly is literary fame. Therefore, he continues the writing of fiction even after his uncle's bequest has made him a millionaire.

Charles Dudley Warner, like Crawford, was attracted by the genteel classes of New York city. Crawford pictured incidents in the lives of the Lauderdale family in his *Katharine Lauderdale* and *The Ralstons,* which will be noticed in other parts of this work, but Warner's trilogy of New York novels will be discussed here because they present clear-cut instances of struggle for success in the city.

In his *A Little Journey in the World,* the first of the trilogy, (1889), Margaret Henderson, coming to New York from the suburb of a small New England city, finds herself fascinated by her new surroundings and the varied round of pleasures which lie before her. Hitherto, she had been an intellectual woman keenly interested in the cultural life of her community, and in its efforts to better the lot of those less fortunate than herself. But in the great city, under the example of a husband who worships at the shrine of money and the power which money brings, she is transformed. Her consuming passion becomes not knowledge or philanthropy but social leadership.

A brilliant opportunity for display comes with the house-warming party which she and her husband give to one thousand guests. The new town house, large enough for a royal court, was embellished with valuable collections of art, curios, and rare books. Margaret as hostess "was regnant." The world appeared to be at her feet, but, in reality, the sumptuous affair marked the completion of her spiritual downfall. This she discovered while she was conversing with the new Earl of Chisholm, a man who many years before had proposed marriage to her when he was just plain John Lynn. She realized on how much higher a plane his life was elevated than hers; and that she had permitted herself to be satisfied with the transient social triumphs of the city, and had neglected to cultivate those spiritual sides of her nature which, in her small-town life, had occupied so much of her attention and had given her so much real joy. She looked upon herself now as a "dead soul" which the city had subdued through its social allurements.

Henderson, her husband, likewise had come to New York from New England.* His rapid rise in the business world was facilitated by unscrupulous practices which caused financial ruin to thousands of unsuspecting investors. He was ranked among the three of four greatest capitalists of the country, whose every movement was noted by telegraph and newspaper. To appease the

---

*Henderson's career is carried through *A Little Journey* and also *The Golden House.*

public and his conscience as well for his sharp dealings, Henderson gave a quarter of a million dollars for a college building in the South and established a fund of $10,000 named the "Margaret Fund" in memory of his first wife, to be used for the relief of some of New York's needy families. Death came suddenly to him as a result of a physical collapse brought on by over-work. We have noted that Hiram Meeker, in one of Kimball's novels, also suffered a break-down in the midst of adding to an enormous fortune. Others could be cited, as for example, Rodman Harvey, the merchant in William H. Bishop's *The House of a Merchant Prince* (1883). The novelists of city life were beginning to sound a note of warning to their millionaire townsmen to cease their high-pressure mode of living and pay more attention to recreation. Henderson's fortune, intended by him to be devoted to the endowment of an industrial school for the East Side, was seized by his second wife, through the simple expedient of destroying the will which contained the provisions for the establishment of the school.

In the second of the trilogy, *The Golden House* (1895), we follow the city career of a younger man, Jack Delancy, whose besetting vice was not avarice, but idleness. With an assured income of $20,000 a year, but without any more ambition than most of his fellow clubmen, Jack was fortunate in marrying Edith Fletcher, a young woman who had a plentiful supply of that moral earnestness which he so woefully lacked. Jack invested some of his money in Henderson's enterprise, but quickly wasted the proceeds therefrom. He had promised his wife to get into a profession but kept putting this off. He was the typical dissipated young clubman of the eighties or nineties—not very bad, but certainly not of much real worth unless aroused by a crisis. For him the crisis comes with the death of Henderson and the complete loss of his fortune and his luxurious home. For a time, Jack goes from bad to worse. He leaves his club and takes rooms in a cheap lodging-house. A sense of shame at his failure keeps him from visiting his family who are now in the country at the Golden House, which fortunately is owned by his wife. After a few months, Mrs. Delancy comes personally to the city, goes to a cousin in the twine business and persuades him to offer Jack a clerkship. Realization that he can earn his own living and support his family restores his confidence in himself. At the end of the novel he and his wife begin a new kind of life on a more solid foundation. They return to the city—to live in a moderate-priced apartment. Jack progresses in his clerkship and receives a more responsible post, but although he had conquered in the struggle with the city, he understands perfectly the difficulties that still lie before him, for memories of the old care-free, dissipated life at the club still persist in coming at times into his mind. His level-headed wife is the only agency to keep him constantly to the straight and narrow path, but now that he has lost his bankroll, her task will not be nearly as difficult as before.

Warner's third novel in this series, *That Fortune* (1899), includes the career of a young girl of calm strength of character who grows up unspoiled amidst the splendors of a magnificent city home. The Mavicks, her parents, were entirely absorbed by their passion for wealth and power, while Evelyn, reared under the supervision of a capable Scotch nurse and governess, lived in a world of idealism. When the panic of 1893 struck New York, she was little troubled, but her parents who suddenly lost everything in life that seemed most desirable to them, were in despair. The novel illustrates the fact that even a millionaire's daughter, living among typical metropolitan surroundings, can escape all the temptations that would tend to make her pleasure-loving, idle, and extravagant. But that the daughter of parents of the caliber of the Mavicks could accomplish such a miracle, even with a minister's daughter as governess, seems more than a little improbable.

Another character in the same novel who is notably successful in the city is the country-reared Philip Burnett, who comes to New York and scores with a novel written after his working hours as clerk in a law-office. *The Puritan Nun* was not accepted entirely on its own merits, for the decision of the head of the publishing house was affected by the following discoveries that he had made about its author: that he stood well in the most prominent law firm in the city; that ladies of established position recognized his talent; that he dined here and there in a good set; and that he belonged to one of the best clubs.* Soon after the publication of his novel,

---

*Warner, Charles D.—"That Fortune", New York, 1899 (edition of 1904, 194.)

Philip received offers from editors for short stories, and was able to give up his clerkship to take a position as publisher's reader. From this he gradually advanced until the same firm had given him a permanent position with time permitted for creative work. His literary success seems rather easily acquired and to have been simplified greatly by a pleasing personality and strong social connections. Allowance should, of course, be made for Warner's customary satire, generally mild, and probably directed here against the ease with which certain young writers of his day climbed to literary fame in New York city.

Much less fortunate is Michael Akershem in his city adventures, as Miss Ellen Glasgow described them in *The Descendant* (1897). He came to New York at the age of nineteen from a small Virginia town. Because he was born of poor stock, the people there had scorned and hated him. He becomes embittered against God and man, an attitude that is intensified by some of the associations that he makes in New York. There he becomes editor of *The Iconoclast,* a reform journal; establishes the radical Iconoclast Society; and lives with Rachel Gavin, an artist as fearless of opinion as he is himself. Good influences are not absent in friends of more conventional habits and beliefs, but he finds greater congeniality with those who are at war with convention, since he was by nature an insurgent even before he came to the city. Final defeat in the struggle against his own tempestuous nature is hastened by his killing of a man who dares to question the morality of his relations with Miss Gavin. He is sentenced to serve ten years in prison, and thus fails in his attempt to escape from the intolerance of his fellow-creatures, because intolerance, he learns, is unfortunately, an essential ingredient of urban, as well as of country, life. The larger opportunities of the city became for him not opportunities for serving his fellow-man, but opportunities for spreading doctrines of bitterness and hate through the medium of a radical press. Thus, the author's picture of the city is a depressing one, owing to her concentration upon its seamy side, which many of her fellow-novelists carefully avoided.

Miss Glasgow soon turned her attention to the South for story material, but another author, Brander Matthews, writing about the same time, devoted himself entirely to New York city. He knew this life thoroughly in all its phases, and his ardent love for it is reflected in popular collections of short stories such as *Vignettes of Manhattan* (1894) and *Outlines in Local Color* (1898), and in his less well known, but almost as successful novels. Two of these, *His Father's Son* (1895) and *A Confident Tomorrow* (1900), contain excellent examples of the success-or-failure motive. After reading the first of them, the reader may very pertinently inquire whether Ezra Pierce, the predatory millionaire, is a success or a failure. The reply depends, of course, upon one's point of view. Successful he certainly was in the acquisition of millions, and in the overthrow of all business rivals who dared to contest his supremacy. But from a broader viewpoint, his life was a complete failure. His blameless home life and his unequalled generosity to his church cannot eliminate from the reader's mind his enormous influence for evil upon his son Winslow. The latter had acquired familiarity with all his father's shady business practices, had learned to speculate on the stock market and even to tamper with certificates. In addition, the temptations of New York club life had made him a drunkard and an unfaithful husband. Thinking to rid himself of immediate responsibility for his son, the father persuaded him to live abroad and gave him a large yearly allowance for that purpose. But Winslow again disgraced the family name by a divorce from his American wife and a marriage to an Australian ballet-dancer. As the curtain is lowered on this domestic tragedy, the son is declared to have written his father for more money, a type of ending that is reminiscent of Howells. Pierce by his complete absorption in business and inability to participate in social or amusement life recalls Hiram Meeker in Kimball's *Was He Successful?* Meeker likewise had no comfort from his son with whom he was continually at odds. The novel of Matthews is, however, much more readable, more vivid, more life-like in characterization, and a moral is not forced upon the reader's attention.

Frank Sartain, the hero of *A Confident Tomorrow*, comes to New York with a manuscript novel in his trunk like Shelley Ray, but he possesses an advantage denied to Ray in that there is a position waiting for him in the city as editor of a subscription book.

His novel, *Dust and Ashes,* is concerned with life in New York, particularly the evils of Wall Street. The reader may judge of its authenticity when he learns that its author's knowledge of the city was gained, for the most part, by a few visits there with his college glee club. The novel does not pass back and forth from publisher to publisher as did Ray's *A Modern Romeo,* but its publication becomes a certainty when Sartain becomes the editor of *The Manhattan,* for what editor could refrain from printing his own brain-child in his own paper? He owed the editorship to the confidence displayed in his powers by Dircks, a radical interested in city and national reform movements. A second novel about New York promises to be better than the first, since it is based upon actual observation of metropolitan life. If we analyze these successes closely, we see that they were hastened by at least one chance or fortunate circumstance, namely, Sartain's gaining the friendship of Dircks. There is not, however, in his case a repetition of fortunate accidents that occurred to Shelley Ray before his ultimate success.*

What impresses one at once after reading all these novels is the predominance in them of young people who come to the city seeking their fortunes. This migration is a continuous procession, gradually increasing in numbers, until it reaches its height in the eighties and nineties. The largest number seek a footing in the literary field—in poetry, journalism, or fiction; a smaller proportion find their places in law, medicine, art, business, and banking. Many succeed, but a few fail and either return to their homes or meet tragic ends in the city. Older men are in the minority. Those whom we do find are pictured as struggling for success in business life. Among them the millionaire is a familiar figure, and it is unusual to find him happy.

In the earlier novels of this group the difficulties offered to the

*Matthews was evidently influenced to some extent in this story by *The World of Chance* of Howells, for whom he had the deepest regard. We see this in slight similarities of plot and of characters. Thus, Dircks may be compared in respect to age and radicalism with Hughes; Vivian may be set off against Kane in that both give valuable advice to the rising young writer. Kane differs in being a true Bohemian, while Vivian, though a litterateur, is a man who moves in the best social circles. Likewise, in *Grandison Mather,* is found the experienced man of letters—Everett St. Marc—and he also gives invaluable assistance to a young novelist.

youthful newcomer seem to be those of the over-grown town and not of the large city as we know it now. Our cities were then, of course, much smaller. For example, New York in 1825 had a population of only 166,000. Success at that time came rather easily, as we saw with young lawyers like Clinton Bradshaw and Archibald Lisle. In the 1860's, when cities became more densely populated and competition keener, our novelists were more emphatic in stressing the vicissitudes of the struggle in the city. Now appeared forcible revelations of wrongs committed in Wall Street and of fortunes made legally and illegally; the new business man made his appearance—only a few years after his appearance in real life.* He is to be found in the novels of Richard B. Kimball who wrote of New York business conditions as they were from 1860-1865. Kimball calls attention to the millionaire who works himself into an early grave. This personage, so characteristic of life in the large city, was carried forward without interruption to the close of the period; good examples of him, besides Kimball's treatment, may be found in Bishop's *The House of a Merchant Prince* (1883); Warner's *A Little Journey in the World* (1889) and *The Golden House* (1895); and Brander Matthews' *His Father's Son* (1895).

In the eighties and nineties the exodus of young men and women from the small towns to the large cities became particularly noticeable. Our novelists, especially Howells, Warner, Matthews, Harland and Miss Glasgow, found congenial topics for their pens in depicting their adventures. The prominence which these writers gave to seekers after literary laurels may be explained partly from the fact that fiction was at the time greatly on the increase, and partly from the fact that they were writing about their own profession, recalling their own days of apprenticeship, the memories of which they now delighted in passing on to their readers in the form of fiction. Howells was most severe in his measure of the qualifications needed for urban success. Not that he delighted in

---

*Theodore Clarke Smith in "Parties and Slavery, 1850-1859", New York, 1906, declares that during the decade, 1850-1859, "the new business man, his whole nature concentrated in competitive production or distribution . . . filled the cities, accompanied the railroads into all corners of the north, and turned into wealth-giving the keenness and vigor of an unexhausted race." (p. 273).

picturing the catastrophies of life in the city, for a study of his novels laid in the city will reveal few scenes of violence or tragedy. The events portrayed by him are the commonplace happenings of every-day life. Since it was common for young aspirants for success in art, literature or journalism to seek the greater opportunities open to them in the large city it was natural that Howells should portray their experiences there. And since these were generally quite devoid of violent incidents, it was natural that Howells' narratives should be so likewise. His theory of realism called for no salacious or sensational events to enliven the unadorned picture of the struggle for recognition. Other writers of the same period employed much the same kind of restraint, influenced in some cases by the example of Howells and in others guided by their own objection to such scenes.

It should be remembered that there existed throughout this period a group of writers who assiduously cultivated the sensational aspects of city life. We have not considered it necessary to trace their efforts in picturing the success-or-failure theme because of the absence of any literary quality in their novels. Some features of their work must of necessity be noted in later chapters. Here we can but inscribe the names of some of them: George Lippard, John T. Irving, P. Hamilton Myers, Joseph H. Ingraham, and Timothy S. Arthur. Their novels were so utterly deficient in style and characterization that they are now almost completely forgotten.

What these men lacked in craftsmanship can, however, be found present to a pleasing degree in the fiction of writers like Miss Sedgwick, Bayard Taylor, William Dean Howells, F. Marion Crawford, Ellen Glasgow, and Brander Matthews. Although not equal in ability, all of the latter group exhibit an excellent style of composition and individuality in character drawing. Howells produced the most noteworthy studies of persons whose lives were notably affected by the city in the creation of characters like Bartley Hubbard, Silas Lapham, and Jeff Durgin. He was likewise the most successful in concentrating attention upon one or two important problems of the urban struggle, thus excluding extraneous material. The others who strove for the same goal fell short of Howells' attainments, because they were often guilty of jumping from one phase of the life of the city to another without sufficient connection.

All the writers of the group just named were conscious of the serious obstacles that the city is accustomed to throw into the path of newcomers who strive to conquer in the life struggle there. It is to their eternal credit that they depicted real human beings engaged in these arduous contests and did not represent them as being universally successful. Some, indeed, had to bow in defeat to the strength of the city forces opposing them. And a majority of the others were victorious only after persistent, courageous fighting.

CHAPTER II

DISASTERS OF CITY LIFE

In this chapter consideration is given to unusual and sensational events—to incidents that could command a prominent position on the first pages of the daily newspaper. Sensation writers are well represented among the recorders of disasters, but their works are unworthy of more than passing mention. They serve merely to indicate the nature of the popular taste that gloried in them. Writers of a higher type of novel artistically did not neglect the field. We find that some of them were interested in describing city-wide disasters like the epidemics of disease that raged in their cities at times within their own recollection. Others described personal and family disasters caused by duelling or intemperance and strove by means of the novel to expose the great evils of those practices. Novels representing poverty in the city also have an interest here, for they often include pictures of tragic situations that were caused directly by the unfortunate urban environment of the persons concerned. Fiction describing villainy merits consideration in this chapter only in so far as the villains therein presented are real and life-like creations. In the majority of the novels of mystery and crime this is not true. Therefore, they are, as a class, disregarded, for they can have but a temporary value, interesting though they sometimes may be, from the standpoint of plot.

City Plagues or Epidemics

Descriptions of city-wide epidemics have an historical interest to the modern reader since they recall conditions which the enormous improvements in municipal sanitation have practically eliminated from American cities. Among these disasters the yellow-fever epidemics in Philadelphia and New York during the last years of the eighteenth century and the early years of the nineteenth century were favorite subjects. None of the later plagues that invaded our Eastern cities seem to have claimed fictional attention.

Charles Brockden Brown lived through the yellow-fever epidemic of New York in 1798; and in *Ormond* and *Arthur Mervyn* he presents his impressions of those tragic days, though he transfers the scene to Philadelphia. Thus in *Ormond* (1799) one reads that to the native citizens of Philadelphia it seemed unreasonable that "the metropolis of her own country—a town famous for the salubrity of its airs and the perfection of its police" could have the yellow fever within its boundaries. People on the streets appeared filled with terror. They were using vinegar as an antidote. Mortality was great. In one alley two hundred persons out of a total of three hundred residents died within three weeks. Only with the coming of cold weather did the plague subside. Then business was quickly restored; streets were again crowded, and theatres were opened, as a company of English comedians made its first appearance in the Quaker City.

A similar account is found in *Arthur Mervyn*. Arthur's experiences in the plague-infested city while searching for Wallace seem unusual and terrifying, but they are confirmed in their main facts by the accounts presented by the historian John B. McMaster based upon a study of first-hand sources. The terror with which the citizens contemplate the disease is matched by their fear of the city hospital at Bush-hill, a veritable death-house. A girl fights against being carried there, for in her mind the hospital is associated with certain death or "the sufferance of every evil which the known inhumanity of its attendants could inflict." Wallace's exposure of conditions at Bush-hill, where he was himself confined for a time, is a fearless indictment. He found the place crowded, with beds scarcely three feet apart, and attendants incredibly negligent, spending most of their time in carousing in the lower apartments of the building. To quote his own words:

"A female visage, bloated with malignity and drunkenness, occasionally looked in. Dying eyes were cast upon her, invoking the boon, perhaps, of a drop of cold water. . . .

"The visitant had left the banquet for a moment, only to see who was dead. If she entered the room, blinking eyes and reeling steps, shewed her to be totally unqualified for ministering the aid that was needed.

Presently she disappeared and others ascended the staircase, a coffin was deposited at the door, the wretch, whose heart still quivered, was seized by rude hands, and dragged along the floor into the passage."*

In *Laura* (1809) misery and suffering as a result of the plague are again emphasized. The heroine, on her way to nurse her lover stricken with the fever, found Philadelphia's streets deserted, its wharves bare of ships, and three-fourths of the houses closed. Dogs, forgotten by owners in the hurry of removal, howled dismally; groans could be heard from dying persons. Carts passed, constantly, loaded with coffins, or carrying "emaciated forms of dying creatures, either motionless extended on the straw, or tearing their hair with frantic gestures and dismal shrieks, endeavoring to escape."†

To a Southern visitor in New York the conduct of the citizens upon an outbreak of the epidemic seems extraordinary, and he comments that over night "the throng, and hurry . . . and pleasure of business, have changed into the throng, and hurry, and misery of fear. . . . The only business which thrives is that of the apothecaries and coffin-makers."‡ After observing these misfortunes wrought by the plague, he is induced to moralize upon the dangers of a city residence and to warn the country youth against venturing into the city unless extremely urgent business brings him there.

Although the writers of these plague episodes introduced them only incidentally as adjuncts to the unfolding of their plots, they form now for the general reader some of the most attractive features of the novels. Brown's descriptions are particularly vivid, indeed, too much so at times, for in their insistence upon exact details of the progress of disease they become revolting. S. Weir Mitchell avoided this fault in *The Red City* (1907), for while he described a plague in Philadelphia in the year 1793, he was careful to exclude too frank reference to the loathsome character of the yellow fever. His account seems as effective as

---

*Brown, Charles Brockden, "Arthur Mervyn", 2 vols., 1799-1800, edition of 1857, Phila., vol. 1, p. 157.
†"Laura, by a Lady of Philadelphia", Phila., 1809, 64.
‡Carruthers, William A.—"The Kentuckian in New York, or The Adventures of Three Southerns, by a Virginian", 2 vols., New York, 1834, vol. 2, 22-23.

Brown's, though, of course, it does not contain the elements of terror and horror which were so prominent in the work of the earlier man.

Duelling

Discussion of duelling in the American novel may be traced as far back as 1792 when H. H. Brackenridge cleverly and effectively satirized it in a special chapter of his picaresque story *Modern Chivalry*. Ironically, he writes that duelling "has produced as great an improvement in manners as the discovery of the load-stone and mariner's compass has in navigation," and . . . "it is a greater aid to government than the alliance of the church and state itself."*

Settlement of disputes by recourse to the duel was a general practice among American gentlemen of the first third of the nineteenth century. Cooper writes that duels were infrequent in the East except in New York city. They were exceedingly rare in New England, but in large cities were about as common as in France or England.† He explains the notion that Americans are great duellists and even semi-barbarians arises partly from excessive publicity given by the thousand journals of the country to the slightest offense against its laws.

Novelists in the 1830's and 1840's and even earlier were directing attention to this ancient institution. Miss Sedgwick notes a changing attitude of New York city in *Clarence, or a Tale of Our Own Times* (1830). Gerald Roscoe, a young attorney in this story, when challenged to personal combat, refuses to meet his opponent because he does not approve of duelling, thinks the enlightened people of New York are opposed to it, and that there is a universal sense against it in New England, and, above all else, because he knows that he is the victim of a plot and has not been guilty of any act that could possibly be judged dishonorable. He is no coward as he proves when his enemies, two in number,

---

*Brackenridge, H. H.—"Modern Chivalry", 2 vols., Phila., 1792, vol. 1, 71.

†Cooper, J. Fenimore—"Notions of the Americans", 2 vols., 1828, v. 2, 297-8.

attack him on the street, armed with a cane. The one whom he throws to the ground touches a secret spring in the cane and thus discharges a dirk into Roscoe's arm, making a slight flesh wound. The two attackers are then overpowered by the brave hero, and bystanders who have witnessed the encounter, cry out strongly against their exhibition of poor sportsmanship. It is clear that they champion Roscoe's courageous methods of defence and disapprove of his opponents' resort to trickery. Justice is upheld even though the one attacked was accused of avoiding participation in an affair of honor.

The distinction here drawn between a worthy and an unworthy cause for engagement in a duel is observed likewise by Fay in his *Norman Leslie.* In this novel the hero answers Count Clairmont's unwarranted and malicious slanders against his honesty at cards, not by recourse to an affair of honor, but by horse-whipping his accuser on the street in front of a large and sympathetic crowd.

Where the cause is deemed worthy, participation in the duel cannot honorably be avoided. In Fay's *Sidney Clifton,* published in 1839, the reader is informed that the hero could not have declined the meeting to which he was challenged except "at the hazard of his being discarded from every respectable and fashionable circle." Social custom, it would appear, sanctioned and preserved the duel, even though it was forbidden by the public authorities.

Another novel by the same author—*Hoboken* (1843)—contains a description of a duel originating in New York, and was written with the avowed purposed of exposing the cruelties of the practice. The quarrel started in one of the city's theatres. The principals were Frank Lennox, a young American officer, and Lieutenant Glendinning of the English army. The latter had insulted Frank's companion, Miss Elton, by leaning forward from his seat in a box adjoining theirs and snatching a rose from her dress. The two men went to Hoboken to settle their differences in the time-honored manner; but when Glendinning fires into the air and apologizes, the incident seems closed. The two become warm friends, and the renewal of trouble between them comes from external agencies, namely, the chiding of Glendinning by fellow officers for having, as they believed, acted dishonorably. A biassed report of the incident in the New York newspapers also helped to anger the English.

Fay pictures Frank's last evening at home—his tearful farewell to parents, sister and friends, who know nothing about the affair of honor to which he is pledged for the coming dawn. Only his mother has a premonition of disaster. One reads of his abrupt departure when all have retired; the accidental meeting of the principals in the Park, at which Frank haughtily refuses the other's offer of apology; the heavy supper with Colonel Randolph, his second, and a young surgeon; Frank's over-indulgence in champagne despite Randolph's repeated warnings that he will need a steady hand; then in the early morning the journey to Hoboken by row-boat, and the landing at daybreak. The rifles are discharged simultaneously, but Frank Lennox is the one to fall, while Glendinning is unhurt. The grief of the parents when the body is brought home—"the conscience-stricken anguish of the father" who had always upheld duelling for his sons, and "the wild shrieks of the mother" we are left to imagine. Mr. Lennox never fully recovers from the shock and has to retire from active business. His wife, having, as the author explains, the support of religion, becomes, after a long time, resigned to her loss.

The case against the duel is here presented chiefly by means of the story, but Fay, fond as always of moralizing, could not wholly restrain from comment. He declares bitterly, "It is fashionable to point at the drunkard the finger of scorn, but the murderer and the duellist, only by chance prevented from becoming one, hears the murmur of interest, of admiration, and applause."*

A writer of a more popular type of fiction, J. H. Ingraham, records a fatal duel in his *Edward Austin: or, The Hunting Flask. A Tale of the Forest and Town* (1842). Again the place is Hoboken; the time is sunset. The principals first use pistols, then turn to swords which prove more effective. The hero is struck through the heart, and thus ends his career of dissipation begun with drinking and gambling in the big city. The short paperbound volume was probably just as adequate a piece of propaganda against the duel as the more elaborately conceived works. With-

---

*Fay, Theodore S.—"Hoboken", New York, 1843, vol. 2, 74.

out permanent merit, it survives for the social historian today as an example of a growing agitation against a national evil.

The efforts of these writers when considered as a whole seem to point to the existence of a two-fold purpose. Miss Sedgwick in *Clarence* and Fay in *Norman Leslie* desire to picture a growing opposition on the part of people of the city towards a rigid code of honor which required every quarrel between gentlemen to be settled by a duel. Fay again in *Sidney Clifton* and *Hoboken,* and Ingraham in *Edward Austin* endeavor to present in forcible, though melodramatic fashion, the horrors of duelling and its cruelties, especially from the standpoint of the bereaved families of those who have been killed.

What part did these novels play in moulding American public opinion against duelling? To answer this, we must examine the work of other agencies besides the novel. An early instance in the drama is J. B. White's tragedy, *Modern Honor* (1812) which was produced at Charleston in an effort to expose the evils of this practice.* The pulpit aided not only by means of the spoken word but also by the printing of sermons and tracts upon the subject. President Andrew Jackson in 1830 put his disapproval upon it by causing the names of four Navy officers to be erased from the rolls for having engaged in duels. Our national periodicals printed occasional articles on duelling, notably: the *North American Review* for April, 1828, which directed attention to its inefficiency and absurdity; the *Democratic Review's* extended notice in September and October, 1842, of Millingen's *History of Duelling;* and the *Knickerbocker Magazine's* discussion of *The Code of Honor,* May, 1851, with emphasis upon the fact that Charles Dickens who denounced so many social evils, was rather lukewarm in regard to the duel, for, while he capably ridiculed it in *Pickwick Papers,* he introduced it into several other of his novels as a necessary part of the life of the times. That American novelists from 1830 to 1843 were working actively for the abolition of the duel has already been noticed. Other novels outside of the field of city life may be added to the list, such as John Neal's *Keep Cool* (1818), and Theodore Fay's *Countess Ida* (1840), a

---

*Quinn, Arthur Hobson—"A History of the American Drama from the Beginning to the Civil War", New York, 1923, 189-190.

story of Berlin life. All of these agencies in combination must have had a marked effect, for even in 1842 (a year before Fay's *Hoboken*) the writer of the *Democratic Review* article already noted could say positively that no one in this country is "under any obligation to accept a challenge. The public opinion will not only fully justify and sustain a noble and conscientious refusal in such a case, but it has little else than contempt, as well as severe censure, for the opposite course."* Miss Sedgwick and Theodore Fay, as we have seen, had worked for the development of just such a state of public opinion, in *Clarence* and *Norman Leslie,* and now that the goal was reached, we may safely conclude that they had played an important part in its attainment. Duelling, however, was not yet completely eradicated. Even though public opinion be aroused against it, a long-sanctioned custom dies slowly in this country, so that it was not until the end of the Civil War that duelling became obsolete.

The duel receives scant attention from novelists writing of city life after the War. One instance is found in *The House of the Merchant Prince.* A controversy between the merchant Rodman Harvey and Fletcher St. Hill terminates in the latter, a younger man, crying out that he desires satisfaction for Harvey's slanders against his reputation. The merchant prince, fearing the use of violence, declares emphatically that the duel is no longer a New York custom and that his age, too, interposes serious obstacles to his participation in it.

Other means of settlement of disputes than by recourse to the duel were discovered to be just as efficacious. Nature's own weapons, the fists, were sometimes used, and also the cane and horse-whip. These were not so liable to result in permanent and irreparable disaster as the duel. The cane, the use of which was noticed in *Norman Leslie,* was still used by gentlemen of the city in the seventies. In Edgar Fawcett's *A New York Family* (1891), a father-in-law avenges the mistreatment of his daughter by stopping his son-in-law on Fifth Avenue and striking him repeatedly over the shoulders with his gold-headed cane and then kicking him into the gutter. The encounter took place in front of a club to

---

Democratic Review, vol. 11, p. 423 (October, 1842).

which the younger man belonged and was, therefore, witnessed by many of his friends who had gathered at the windows attracted by the clamor on the sidewalk. The outcome of the affair was disastrous in that it led to temporary disgrace for the beaten man and his ousting from all the clubs to which he belonged, but, of course, there was no loss of life.

Abolition of duelling did not result in the cessation of gun-play in the cities. Indeed, the duel with its formal code and its guarantee to each contestant of a fair shot may well be regarded as superior to the later practice of shooting one's enemy at sight or from ambush. Many novels involving murders were laid in the city. For instance, there was *A Tragic Mystery* (1887) by Julian Hawthorne. Another of higher literary quality was Miss Glasgow's *The Descendant,* which was mentioned in the previous chapter. In this the author pictures Michael Akershem's dispute with Kyle, his assistant editor; the latter's insulting remarks; and Akershem's killing of the man without warning and without permitting him to defend himself or to retract his words.

Intemperance

Although the temperance movement did not become nation-wid : until 1850-1855, total abstinence societies date as far back as 1808. By 1833 the New York State Temperance Society could report that it had 1158 auxiliary societies with 161,721 members, or at least one in thirteen of the entire state population.* The Quarterly List of New Publications printed by the *North American Review* showed a steady output of temperance tracts and sermons during the thirties and forties. Prohibition was considered by several states, but Maine was the first to pass a state law stopping the manufacture and sale of intoxicating liquors, in 1851. Temperance novels began to increase rapidly in the fifties. Most popular was T. S. Arthur's *Ten Nights in a Bar Room* (1852), which was rural in setting. It narrated in lurid fashion the domestic calamities wrought in the pleasant village of Cedarville by a tavern called the "Sickle and Sheaf."

North American Review, vol. 36, p. 189 (Jan. 1833).

The temperance movement had always strong rural support. By 1878 four rural states had adopted state-wide prohibition, namely, Maine, New Hampshire, Vermont, and Kansas. And women from rural districts were the founders of the Women's Christian Temperance Union in 1874. The greatest tasks of the temperance workers were not, however, to be found in the rural environment but in the large cities. There the working man was in the habit of seeking the saloon immediately after his day's work, and a large immigrant population persisted in maintaining family drinking customs learned in the homeland. For the man of social distinction the club or lodge provided similar attractions to those which the laborer found in his tavern.*

Examples of individuals in a large city suffering disaster or near-disaster as a result of excessive drinking are found in George W. Curtis's *Trumps*,† and in Bayard Taylor's *John Godfrey's Fortunes*. Both of these are laid in New York city. In the former, Abel Newt, son of a commission merchant, has caused his father's failure by personal extravagances and impractical notions for the conduct of the business. He is avaricious and unscrupulous; his campaign for representative in Congress is successful despite the fact that he was found intoxicated on two critical occasions: first, when he was being serenaded by party-workers, and second, when he was slated for a conference with the party leaders. In Congress he is the tool of a group of politicians interested in the passage of a land grant bill; he becomes intimate with a notorious woman lobbyist from New York and plans to sail to Europe with her. In order to obtain sufficient funds for the trip he forges his uncle's signature thus gaining $100,000 but loses most if it in a New York gambling den. Afterwards he enters a saloon, where he becomes so overcome by liquor that he quarrels with three of his own political henchmen whom he does not recognize, and is killed. The drink habit cannot be blamed for all of Newt's misfortunes, but it would seem that Curtis was desirous of showing that an intoxicated person is liable at the most unexpected moment to meet his doom. It is clear too that the author

---

*Schlesinger, Arthur M.—"The Rise of the City, 1878-1898", New York, 1933, 353.

†*Harper's Weekly*, April 9, 1859, to Jan. 21, 1860, and in book form, 1861.

desired to associate together three vices: political graft, gambling, and drinking.

Bayard Taylor provides his readers with a close approach to tragedy in John Godfrey's gradual downward tread in New York city after the disappointment of his love affairs. But even in his worst dissipations he is a sympathetic figure. He has formed the habit of joining other Bohemians in hilarious evenings at the popular Cave of Trophonius. One night finds him there alone, without position, without lodging, and without a great deal of self-respect. Disaster is imminent, but he hears familiar footsteps outside coming nearer and nearer. An inner voice calls to him to rise and go to meet them. He does so, and standing outside of the café, he hears distinctly the footsteps of his boyhood chum Bob Simmons. The latter in passing the Cave sees John, takes him home and shelters him for the night. The next day Bob succeeds in reviving Godfrey's sense of self-esteem and persuades him to return to the newspaper position from which in a moment of pique he had resigned. Thenceforth, his fortunes are on a rising scale until the usual happy reunion of hero and heroine in the final chapter. The pictures of Godfrey's dissipations—mainly drinking and gambling—into which he was led by bad companionship, are vivid and thought-provoking without being sentimental; they are not punctuated by moral preachments as frequently was the case with fiction dealing with intemperance.

In each of the novels just mentioned intemperance plays an impressive but minor role. The main interest lies elsewhere. But with T. S. Arthur's companion piece to his *Ten Nights in a Bar Room,* namely, *Three Years in a Man Trap* (1872), we come to a city novel whose entire purpose is to consider the temperance problem. Like most of this author's novels, it is pure propaganda, aimed, in this case, at the enormous evils of the liquor trade in a large city. Philadelphia is the city represented, though it is not specifically named. It presents the narrative of the three years' experience of a partner in the "Retreat." Episode after episode is heaped upon the reader illustrating calamities traceable directly to the man-trap. The narrator, Hiram Jones, himself temperate in habits, becomes more and more dissatisfied with his connection with the selling of liquor. Tom Lloyd, the other partner, develops into a hopeless drunkard who neglects his family and brutally injures habitués of the saloon when they arouse his anger. Jones stifles his conscience until punishment comes with imprisonment for sixty days for being found guilty of keeping the "Retreat" open on Sundays. Lloyd, jailed for an assault upon a drunkard, suffers an attack of delirium tremens, horribly detailed by the novelist, and dies in agony. When the now repentant Jones is released, he abandons the saloon business for all time and joins a temperance association.

This novel has an air of reality except that the language of the more serious situations is forced and melodramatic. Exaggeration, of course, is present, some of which may be excused by the author's intense passion to curb a great evil. He does not, as a rule, over-indulge in moralizings but confines his sermons within the dialogues of the characters. Of these, some are convincing, though overburdened with statistics; others are too extensive.

One does not always feel the existence of the city in Arthur's novel, for at times the saloon seems a world of its own. What city life is significant is found in temperance meetings at the State House; in description of the activities of a temperance league organized to offset the evils of the "Retreat"; and in depressing pictures of deplorable conditions at the county jail.

Statistics are plentiful in the novel as to the strength of city liquor traffic; thus, one reads that there are two hundred drinking saloons within an area of four or five blocks, and that between sixty and eighty thousand persons frequent saloons every night. But more forcible than cold figures in proving the predominance of the barroom in the city's life are those episodes in the novel which reveal it as an evening attraction for men, young men, and even boys, where they can gather to play cards, dominoes, bagatelle, or other seemingly harmless games. For private parties, upstairs room are available. Boys are admitted, though this was illegal. Arthur shows by examples how boys learned at the "Retreat" vices such as obscene language, gambling, and drinking which often led to their ultimate moral ruin.

Indirectly, the "Retreat," which with Arthur stands for a typical city tavern, had deleterious effect upon the families of men who were its customers. Their wives, sons and daughters suffered.

To name a few of many instances: relapse into an old habit caused one reformed drunkard to kill his wife, then himself; a daughter died of exposure to the cold because of her father's participation in the liquor business; a son, hurt after a bout of drinking when taken home by the bartender, fell heavily just inside the threshold, suffered brain concussion, and thereafter was fitted only for light employment.

Temperance is depicted by Arthur as gaining strength within the city. One notes its effective work in a large bindery, where all hard drinkers are induced to sign the pledge. It is also shown responsible for the enforcement of the Sunday-closing law.

Mrs. Stowe in *We and Our Neighbors* (1873) shows an interest in most of the contemporary problems of the city including that presented by intemperance. A visit to the slums of New York is described; a city mission managed by a Methodist minister is shown serving hot soup to men and women assembled by its superintendent from near-by saloons, bucket-shops and dance-houses. All these places are sketchily represented, and the social system is denounced that permits their existence "within sounds of hundreds of church bells of every denomination." She comments too on "the selling of that poisoned liquor which brings on insanity worse than death; which engenders idiocy, and certainty of vicious propensities in the brain of the helpless unborn infant; which is the source of all the poverty, and more than half the crime, that fills almshouses and prisons, and of untold miseries and agonies to thousands of families."* The story itself contains no disasters to its characters caused directly or indirectly by intemperance; criticism is the only attention which Mrs. Stowe here gives to it.

H. C. Bunner in *The Midge* (1886) emphasized some possible pleasant features of saloon life in his idealized picture of a small, quiet beer-saloon in down-town New York, a place which resembled a club-room more than it did the usual noisy saloon. It was kept by Madame Pigault, a French woman, and named after her the Brasserie Pigault. Regular visitors came every evening to play dominoes. To many men without families it was like home.

---

*Stowe, Mrs. Harriet B.—"We and Our Neighbors", Boston, 1873, 420.

It resembled those French cafés where families spend entire evenings over one or two small glasses of wine. Those who came there were artists, reporters, widowers, bachelors, and on rare occasion, Father Dube, "big, ponderous, and genial." He came to play dominoes with Dr. Peters. Bunner emphasizes the fact that no untoward incidents ever occured there.* But within a very few years Pigault's had changed completely from a brasserie into an American saloon. A younger element, hilarious at times, had usurped the places of the older and Bohemian group who formerly came night after night "to drink mild potations of beer and play long games of dominoes." Mme. Pigault was no longer present. A pool-table provided recreation. Dr. Peters found there "a general deterioration, moral and material." The author now has no defence for it and the reader can, if he wishes, vision it as being gradually converted into another "Retreat" or "Sickle and Sheaf," where disasters can occur without restraint.

A Man's Will by Edgar Fawcett (1888) was very evidently written as propaganda, and takes on at times the semblance of a tract for total abstinence. But it is superior to the usual temperance novel, being written in a more restrained, dignified style. The novel has more unity than Arthur's work, which is little more than a collection of episodes illustrative of disasters in the families coming under the "man trap's" influence. In *A Man's Will,* one family provides the center about which the action moves. First, the elder Saltonstall, head of a private banking firm, succumbs to the habit, against which he has been fighting, with the aid of his wife, for many years. His death occurs in a struggle with the proprietor of a Third Avenue saloon, and in the presence of his son (then only a boy). The boy had already signed a pledge not to drink intoxicating liquors at the earnest solicitation of his

---

*Cf. Paul L. Ford's *The Honorable Peter Sterling,* where Sterling in a letter to his mother describes the saloon in New York as "the poor man's club", where he goes for his social enjoyment and where there is little intemperance. In another discussion he amplifies this statement by expressing a fervent wish for the abolition of all tippling. "But till that day come . . . I want to see fair play. The rich man can lay in a stock of wine, or go to a hotel or club, and get what he wants at any time and at all times. It is not fair, because a man's pockets are filled with nickels instead of eagles, that he shall not have the same right. For that reason, I have always spoken for the saloon." (p. 341).

mother and sister. This he breaks in his second year at Columbia College during a student mock-burial ceremony. Edmund thereafter drinks more moderately until after he has settled down in business and has married. Then as a club-man and as a favorite in social circles he indulges in regular and heavy drinking. Disgrace comes at a private dinner in his own home when servants have to be summoned to carry him unconscious to his room. Failure in business, loss of all his own and his mother's money increase his troubles. Fearing to face his family, he does not go home but takes refuge in a Bowery hotel, where delirium tremens brings him close to death. By a fortunate coincidence, a doctor skilled in this disease is at hand to bring him safely through, and when he returns home, he finds wife forgiving and mother overjoyed at his recovery, and his creditors merciful, so that he can begin life anew. It is a fortunate escape for him—one dictated possibly by the supposed necessity for happy endings in works of fiction.

Artistically, the novel suffers from too obvious thrusting forward of its thesis. For the present-day reader, it is significant as part of a continuous fictional interest in temperance that began before the Civil War, and for its faithful, contemporaneous record of excessive drinking indulged in by college undergraduates residing within a large city and by members of the city's fashionable clubs. It reveals other city habits, too, as, for example, the universality of the practice of serving wines and liquors at social functions. Champagne was almost essential. At one function its absence caused considerable confusion among the men guests, leading them to utter very uncivil growls and a few oaths—all because they had to be satisfied with claret and sherry. Fawcett takes advantage of such conduct to charge New Yorkers with manners "notorious for graceless crudity."

F. Marion Crawford has studied carefully another young man who, like Edmund Saltonstall, was a member of a New York family of high social rank and found himself handicapped by a thirst for liquor. This is John Ralston whose career is outlined in *Katharine Lauderdale* (1894) and *The Ralstons* (1895). The fact that he is potential heir to a portion of the Lauderdale millions, does not prevent his acquiring a sinister reputation through habits of drinking and outbursts of boisterous spirits at inopportune moments. But he is strong, brave, and chivalrous, so that when he confesses to Katharine the hold that liquor has over him, she marries him notwithstanding. His great trial comes on an unlucky day when his every act seems destined to foil his endeavors to maintain a condition of sobriety. Beginning with accidental collisions with club-mates, one after the other, caused by his own haste and clumsiness, but ascribed by the injured parties to his drunkenness, John passes through a succession of trying situations lasting throughout the day. He has taken but half a glass of whiskey which has not affected his senses at all, but millionaire Uncle Robert, noticing it on his breath, accuses him of having drunk to excess. A quarrel results, after which John rushes out of his relative's house without his coat and with hat badly damaged where his uncle had struck it. As he walks thus through the city streets on a cold winter night, he makes a most disreputable appearance, and this is greatly increased when he falls at full length over building material piled upon the side-walk. He strikes his head; his senses become confused and he wanders aimlessly. When his mind clears, he finds himself in Tompkins Square from which he takes a horse-car for home, but once inside the conveyance he falls asleep from exhaustion. When awakened at the end of the route by a short, broad-shouldered man with thick neck, he fights him and is knocked unconscious. Policemen take him home apparently intoxicated. Even his mother believes him drunk until the family doctor after examination pronounces him perfectly sober but suffering from a slight concussion of the brain. The newspapers carry sensational reports the next morning of the incident in which as they retell it, "Mr. R., a well-known young gentleman about town and the hero of more than one midnight adventure at last met his match in the person of Tom Shelton, the famous light-weight pugilist." Public vindication comes that evening when at a dinner party John narrates his strange adventures and clears himself of the charge of overindulgence. This is a highly idealistic treatment of the problem and the narrative though improbable is impressive in its verge upon the tragic and by reason of its entertaining style.

We have considered here only a few of many novels that tried to show what was well-known: that many lives in our large Eastern cities were being ruined by intemperance. Temperance novels, sentimental or melodramatic in character, multiplied greatly from the 1850's on to the close of the century. T. S. Arthur was especially prolific of this type of propaganda fiction. The popular paper-back novels were filled with examples of heavy drinking. Not primarily written to preach intemperance, they did effective work by associating in their readers' minds the common habit of drink with the more criminal habits of gambling, thievery, and immorality. All of these were described in that haven of wickedness, the city. An example is J. H. Ingraham's *Edward Austin* already mentioned in connection with duelling. In that novel the principal character, a city youth, is addicted to gambling and drinking which lead eventually to a fatal duel.

Continuous repetition on the part of some of our novelists of episodes exhibiting evils of the intemperate life as found in the large cities must have played an important part in the growth of the temperance movement there. But propaganda dominated their efforts so thoroughly that no outstanding works from a literary standpoint were produced. This is explained by the fact that an ardent propagandist in fiction such as T. S. Arthur has little if any regard for the artistic possibilities of his medium. Generally, he is a hasty craftsman who thinks that his enormous output will amply compensate for the absence of real quality in his work. Not content to let the story carry its own moral, he thrusts his own personality into the narrative by means of his oft-repeated comments and thus gains either the hostility of his readers or bores them to distraction.

From city novels belonging to the higher type of literature, one may select here and there impressive episodes illustrating the harmful effects of excessive drinking. The brief attention given to intemperance in comparison with other problems of the city does not detract from its effectiveness, because the episodes are developed objectively and as part of the story. But the efforts of the professional temperance writers suffered from a tendency to overload the reader with calamities all ascribed to one common cause. Life in a large city is more complex than that. Therefore, Edgar Fawcett achieved a closer approximation to literature in *A Man's Will* than did T. S. Arthur in his *Three Years in a Man Trap*, for although Fawcett mingled his drinking incidents with generous slices from other phases of city life and inserted a few dashes of humor as seasoning, Arthur confined himself entirely to one phase, the liquor situation, and made no attempt to relieve the tension with humor. More effective than the work of either of these men are the scattered intemperance pictures provided by Curtis, Taylor, and Crawford in novels above noted. These men did not allow their artistic sensibilities to be carried away by the city's vast problems but alloted to each the attention which its importance seemed to warrant, and presented it in as impersonal a manner as possible. With them, the story and character development always occupied first place in their thoughts and all didactic elements were made subordinate.

Poverty

One of the earliest fictional treatments of poverty in the city is found in *Monima: or The Beggar Girl*, written in 1803. At the opening of the story Monima and her old father are in a very miserable condition bordering upon starvation. The reader's pity is aroused as Monima goes to Philadelphia looking for work as seamstress. Madame Sontine, for whom she has worked in the past, now has nothing for her but becomes her bitter persecutor. Sally, with whom she and her father stayed when the yellow fever raged in the city, accosts her on the street and presents her with some potatoes, a gift which Monima is reluctant to accept since it is charity. After a few days she suffers her first misfortune from Madame Sontine when she is carried off to the City Workhouse charged with breaking the peace. The brother of Madame, a city watchman, is her coadjutor in these plots against the girl. Bail being provided by a friend, Monima is released. Again starvation threatens, and she is about becoming reconciled to begging on the streets; but relief comes when a ten dollar bill is providentially thrust through the house door. Incidentally, it is a curious fact that Monima, the beggar girl, never practices her profession and never lives up to her name, somewhat to the disappointment of the reader who may have been attracted to the book by its title. Further plots against Monima include confinement in a haunted house and commitment to an insane asylum, situations that are somewhat reminiscent of the Gothic romance. At the close of the novel, Monima's brother returns home from France, bringing the welcome news that he has recovered the family's valuable French possessions, and that now they are rich. The story is disappointing as a picture of city life and is really not adequately representative of any kind of life.

Monima and her father escaped being drawn into crime because of their impoverished state, but in many of the novels of city life poverty and crime go hand in hand. One finds this, for example in J. T. Irving's *The Attorney* (1842). In this novel Wilkins, one of the accomplices of the villainous attorney, Bolton, is shown journeying to "that portion of the city lying between Chatham and Centre streets . . . in the heart of the region where thieves and cut-throats were skulking to avoid the vigilance of the police and had common lot with the penniless and homeless who came there only to die." Wilkins lives in a room in a cheap, wooden house in the Bowery, near Chatham Square. Here there is poverty, but owing to his wife's care, there is also cleanliness. Lucy Wilkins loves her husband; but he is cruel and fails to appreciate her worth, and desires, in fact, to divorce her so as to marry a rich widow. He abuses Lucy so much that she at last takes shelter on the streets and is found almost dead in front of the steps of an up-town mansion. There she is rescued and receives kind attention and a permanent home. She still remains loyal to her worthless, faithless husband; but he will not listen to her entreaties when meeting him on the street she desires him to break off his dangerous alliance with Bolton. As a result the girl pines away—even the best of medical attention cannot save her—for she has nothing more to live for, now that she knows that Wilkins is lost to her forever. Poverty is not the main but the contributing cause of this domestic tragedy. It led Lucy's husband to shelve her for a richer companion who, he thinks, can make his later years easy ones for him. Poverty also can be blamed for his criminal alliances. The final outcome for Wilkins is madness, murder of the attorney, and his own death in exile at his mother's home in the country thirty miles away. The whole is a sordid, melodramatic tale relieved now and then by touches of humor somewhat in the manner of Charles Dickens.

In the works of George Lippard, the poor are honest, and do not as a rule yield to the temptations of crime. With him, it is the rich who commit the crimes and the poor who are the victims. Their sufferings, in many cases, are a direct result of fraud practiced upon them by wealthy bankers. In *The Quaker City,* for example, Job Joneson, president of a recently-closed bank, is represented as apparently being undisturbed by the institution's failure. He continues to maintain his magnificent town house and his expensive carriage. But when John Davis, a mechanic who has lost $600 in Joneson's bank, and is out of work, and has a daughter lying at the point of death, appeals to him for financial aid, the banker flatly refuses him. Early the next morning the Bank President is punished for this lack of charity, for while returning from a party at Deacon Roger's home where he had taken too much wine, he was stricken with apoplexy. His coachman takes him into the nearest house which, by a coincidence all too common in fiction, proves to be the home of the Mechanic, who now lies there dead (a suicide) and his daughter also. Lippard comments:

"The legalized Robber lay beside the wretch whom he had plundered. The well-fed Bank President, who not ten hours past, had refused the starving Mechanic one solitary dollar, now lay beside the victim of his lawful fraud, like that victim, a loathsome mass of clay, on which worms would soon hold their revel."*

Unfortunately the author permits his prejudice against the rich to overpower his sense of fairness. No doubt, the poor were victimized then as they are today; but Lippard would teach us that there were no exceptions to the plunder of the poor by the rich, a condition of affairs which is unbelievable.

Crime and poverty are again linked in the revelations of professional begging on city streets contained in novels by J. T. Irving and T. S. Arthur. In Irving's *Harry Harson* (1844) the reader is introduced to a Mrs. Blossom who makes a living

---

*Lippard, George, "The Quaker City; or The Monks of Monk Hall," Phila., 1844, 349.

out of sending children on the streets each day to beg. She posts them herself and watches from a distance as they greet the passers-by. Mr. and Mrs. Snork are in the same business. Their most prized decoy, the one who yields them the largest returns, is a girl who can become sick ten times in one afternoon. She is worth at least $2 a day to them until the House of Refuge takes her. Remembering J. T. Irving's fondness for Dickens and his frank imitation of that master's style, one cannot help but believe that he was here inspired by *Oliver Twist*. Fraudulent solicitation is a common practice in large cities. Another example is found in Arthur's *Cast Adrift* (1873), where among other almost incredible features of New York life in the slums, one finds women trafficking in young babies to be used by them as decoys for pennies. The child is obtained by theft or is purchased from a mother by whom it is unwanted. The baby thus obtained is carried in the arms of the new owner as she begs on street corners. The more puny the child, the more productive it is likely to be to the beggar. In this story, a mother, Edith Dinnefort, thinks that she recognizes her own child in the arms of one of these creatures. The child had been reported to her as dead, but in reality it had been given by the grandmother to a woman who, for $50, agreed to take and rear it.

Horror equal to that which strikes upon the senses of the reader in imagining this traffic in babies is aroused in his reading of conditions of poverty and starvation so uncompromisingly reported in Joaquin Miller's *The Destruction of Gotham* (1886). In this fantastic story one is reminded again of the distasteful pictures of loathsome disease and death that were found in the yellow fever episodes of Brockden Brown. With Miller the details are less excusable, for one feels that he could have created the impression of city wretchedness just as well without them. One scene which may be designated the "horror of horrors" describes the tenement of Dottie Lane where she and her child are threatened by rats as they lie in bed. To keep them away from the child, tobacco stems have been placed around her side of the bed; it was thought that the rats would not eat through the tobacco. Another scene shows Dottie dead, apparently of starvation, and the child just barely alive.

The destruction of the city is engineered by a mob of the poor who overthrow the grandest homes on Fifth Avenue, get desperately drunk at the Brunswick Hotel and then set the whole city afire. Miller is as vehement in denunciation of the rich as was Lippard before him, and like Lippard he believes that the city's poor have always been victimized. He says boldly that the one commandment thought by New Yorkers to be more important than anything else in life is this: "Thou Shalt Not Be Poor!" In another sentence he speaks of "the crime of poverty, the violation of the first great law of the great drunken, reveling, and riotous city."

Edward W. Townsend's *A Daughter of the Tenements* (1895) presents an entirely different possibility of family disaster as the result of poverty, namely, the custom of charitable societies taking children from their parents when they cannot properly support them through lack of money. Teresa Cesarotti, the ballet girl in this novel, suffers a severe accident that necessitates her removal to the hospital. Before leaving the theatre she instructs her friend, Maggie Lyon, to take her child and care for it in some way herself, for she wishes to keep it out of the clutches of the "Society." Townsend regards this attitude as representative of the common belief of the poorer classes. He declares sarcastically:

"Being poor, they can have no such natural love for their offspring as would prompt resentment against any interference by the Society in their relations with their children. That, I say, is what one would reasonably and properly suppose. But the poor are unreasonable and not infrequently improper . . . sometimes so sinfully unreasonable as to love their children, or at least affect to, as much as if they were creatures of refinement and education, and had power enough to take other people's children away from them."*

More cheerful pictures of life among the destitute of a great city can be found in *The Midge* (1886), by H. C. Bunner, and in *The Honorable Peter Sterling,* by P. L. Ford (1894). In both a hand of mercy comes to the aid of homeless and suffering children. In the first, a dying widow entrusts Dr. Peters, a

---

*Townsend, Edward W.—"A Daughter of the Tenements", New York, 1895, 25-26.

curious mixture of physician and priest, with her child, a girl, whom he adopts and rears in his own home. He, of course, falls in love with her but cheerfully acquiesces to her marriage with a promising young artist of about her own age.

Other novelists who are particularly interested in philanthropy among the city poor often give the reader brief sketches of desperate situations in the lives of such families. Thus Charles D. Warner in *The Golden House* (1895) uses vignettes of East Side New York life as suggestive contrasts to his pictures of the splendors of life in the Fifth Avenue sections. This interest in the East Side is reflected not so much in disasters of poverty to be found there as in the personalities of two welfare workers— Dr. Ruth Leigh and Father Damon. Theirs, a true charity, contrasts sharply with showy but insincere efforts such as those of Carmen Henderson, who visits the East Side purely out of curiosity and never inconveniences herself while so doing.

In like manner, novelists of the latter part of the century often involved their discussions of life among the poor with the kindred problems of sincere and insincere philanthropy. It was a favorite topic for their satirical pens.

For a final suggestion of the association together of poverty and sin one may turn to a novel written only a few years before the close of the period—Hamlin Garland's *Jason Edwards* (1897). The Edwards family live in the dirt and squalor of Pleasant Avenue in Boston. They themselves are able to avoid participation in crime, though the wretchedness of their surroundings causes them to move westward to a land of promise, where, according to the railroad posters read by the head of the family, people have homes of their own and cows and trees and do not live "all cooped up in dens" like their city tenement. Their subsequent disillusionment after moving to the prairies has no connection with city life, but there are certain passages in the first part of the novel that seem to suggest the author's belief that nothing good can possibly come out of Boston's Pleasant Avenue or similar wretched streets. In a description of the Avenue at five o'clock on a hot day, he notes the "children, ragged, dirty, half-naked and ferocious," swearing and screaming "in high-pitched, unnatural, animal-like voices, from which all childish music was lost." He notes "frowzy women walking with a gait of utter weariness, aged women, bent and withered, and young women straggling along the sidewalks, laden with parcels, pitifully small, filled with food."* Inside the tenements he pictures other women leaning from the open windows to get a breath of cooler air, "frowns of pain on their faces", while invalids unable to reach the windows to escape the heat and smell of the cooking, turn to the wall, "dumbly praying for death to end their suffering."* Further, Garland forecasts the almost inevitable and hideous future of young people brought up in such an environment—in hot unwholesome alleys "swarming with vicious and desperate life"—alleys which were badly-lighted, poison-tainted and vice-infected. He calls attention through Walter Reeves, his young journalist, to the fact that there were miles of such streets in Boston. The impression left upon the reader of the sordidness of poverty in the city and its almost certain federation with crime is a vivid one painted with all the author's powers of realism.

In the treatment of city disasters caused by poverty one may note certain novelists emphasizing similar facts. J. T. Irving, T. S. Arthur, and Hamlin Garland were all impressed by the circumstance that poverty and crime were often boon companions, and that perhaps poverty was a prime cause of many city crimes. The first two used poverty as part of their plots, representing it by the lives of some of their characters; while with Garland poverty was represented descriptively, rather than through the narrative.

The honesty of the poor was impressed upon the minds of other novelists like Lippard and Joaquin Miller. They—and many others could be found with similar outlook—emphasized the fact that the poor were made innocent victims of the wicked and unscrupulous rich. Unfortunately, their treatments of poverty were marred by their fanatical hatred of the rich as a class which prevented them from understanding that the rich were not always wicked any more than that the poor were always virtuous. Their pictures of the economic classes of society as found in the city were, in a word, too one-sided.

Kind treatment of the city poor was pictured by some novelists

---

*Garland, Hamlin—"Jason Edwards", New York, 1897, 24-5.

who showed that philanthropy sincerely practiced would relieve many of the most tense situations in the lives of these people. Their episodes dealing with poverty were generally marked by an optimism that was in marked contrast with the pessimism of those writers who seemed to delight in depicting the cruelties and horrors of poverty and whose efforts at times resembled the most terrifying products of the Gothic school of fiction.

Villainy

Villainy flourished in the earlier periods of the American novel. The city villain found many victims and caused many disasters. In the hands of sub-literary or sensational novelists he became a ruffian without redeeming qualities; literary artists made him more subtle. With the growth of the novel the blackguard tended to acquire a few redeeming qualities and thus become more human.

Ormond and Welbeck, creations of the brain of Charles Brockden Brown, head the list of villains, if they are taken in chronological sequence. Ormond's career in the Russian army, brief mention of which is made in the novel, was productive of so many killings that his later experiences in Philadelphia and vicinity seem mild in comparison. He is not the conventional villain of Brown's time. He is credited with vast political projects that are "likely to possess an extensive influence on the future conditions of the Western World." Regeneration of mankind is one of them. He is a man of high ideals, who, unfortunately, does not balk at using the most depraved and criminal stratagems to attain his ends.

Welbeck, the patron of Arthur Mervyn, is more closely identified with the city. He possesses little of the glorified ambitions of Ormond, but there is enough of power and mystery about his personality to attract the loyalty of an unsophisticated country lad like Arthur. His villainy includes violation of a sacred promise made to a dying man and fraudulent use of money belonging to the common people who have entrusted him with it. His schemes are not confined to the city, though they emanate therefrom. By posing as a man of wealth with a magnificent home and a large corps of servants, he gains the people's confidence, but when they find themselves the victims of fraud, they learn to hate him. Many others would have suffered too if the city had not stepped in and confined him within debtor's apartments in the Prune Street jail, where he succumbed to a lingering illness. Neither Welbeck nor Ormond is a realistic figure. Both are idealized portraits of social reformers who regard the use of any methods, even the most criminal, as justifiable in furthering their visionary schemes.

Theodore Fay introduces a foreign villain into New York life in the person of Count Clairmont (*Norman Leslie*). Typical of the villain of romance, Clairmont bullies the weak, slanders gentlemen's characters, fakes a marriage ceremony, deserts his mistress, abducts an innocent girl, and contrives to involve Norman Leslie in an accusation of murder.

Michael Rust in J. T. Irving's novel *Harry Harson* is a villain whose life is dominated by greed for money. He has no broad vision for using his money to benefit mankind as had Brown's two villains, but is completely evil in nature, except for a few remnants of affection centering about his daughter Ellen. Though he dwells in a building near Wall Street occupied for the most part by lawyers, Rust has no legal connections and no real civic or community interests, but his career is bound up with the small band of desperadoes over whom he exercises despotic control. They are the outlaws of the city who make their living by preying upon its innocent citizens. They specialize in kidnapping, but Rust himself does not hesitate at murder. His killing of his daughter's seducer seems justified, until it is remembered that he was himself guilty of just such a crime against the daughter of a former ally. Irving's treatment of Rust lowers the novel to the realm of the sensational from which it is only raised at intervals by the inclusion of scenes centering about the genial Harry Harson and his associates.

Melodramatic and sentimental as Irving's work is, Lippard's *The Quaker City* is more so, but that it suited the reading public is proved by the fact that within five years after its first publication, it had passed through twenty-seven editions. Gus Lorimer, the villain and seducer of the heroine, was drawn from real life. His counterpart was a fashionable young libertine who had recently been killed by another Philadelphian for seducing his sister.* Neither this novel nor its companion. *The Empire City* (1853) is worthy of bearing the title which it does, for the city life pictured therein is far from being typical of Philadelphia or New York life of the age represented.

The city villain was not always a man, as may be seen in Miss Cummins' *The Lamplighter* (1854), where Nan Grant causes a girl eight years of age to be thrust into the streets to shift for herself. The banishment is a climax to a long succession of beatings which the child had received at her hands. Nan's part in the story is not important after the first few pages, but judging from what is presented there of her character, one does not hesitate in placing her among the other villains here assembled. The novel itself, except for Nan, is complacent in nature, for as soon as the story turns to tranquil city scenes connected with the old lamplighter's rescue of the outcast girl and her subsequent spiritual growth, villainy is forgotten.

Densdeth, the evil genius of Theodore Winthrop's *Cecil Dreme* (1862), resembles one of those powerful personalities met with in Charles Brockden Brown. In his well-constructed portrait we can see the touch of one who, if he had survived the Civil War, might easily have equalled or excelled the work of that earlier artist. Densdeth cannot be appreciated from the mere perusal of his deeds, for it was his influence upon his associates that marked him apart from the ordinary villain. When one analyzes this magnetism of his, one sees that with it he can do more harm than the most notorious killer. Young Byng appraises him as an "Apostle of Disenchantment", one who reveals evil everywhere. He captivates Byng and yet terrifies him, so that in a curious way Byng finds himself acknowledging "a hateful love for his society." Densdeth serves as sponsor for the young idlers of the city. When he comes into their club in the morning, the loungers lose their air of nonchalance, and the billiard players leave their games. All eagerly crowd about their idol to hear what new scandal he has to bring them and what "new man to jeer or woman to flout." Though pretending to be bored, he is no doubt engaged in just that occupation in which he most relishes. One must

*Oberholtzer, Ellis P.—"The Literary History of Philadelphia", 1906, 265.

believe, too, that he boasts to himself that he has paralyzed the soul of that man of fine genius, Raleigh. The latter jests about this, as in Byng's room in Chrysalis College (an old Gothic structure still used by New York University) he glances at an ancient medieval tapestry representing Purgatory and Hell. Coolly he identifies Densdeth as the devil of the tapestry and himself as one of his victims. Such a poisoner of character was Densdeth and baneful indeed must have been his influence among his city associates.

The great danger which a novelist faces in describing city villainy, or any villainy for that matter, is that he will make it into pure melodrama. Fay, Irving, and Lippard succumbed to this temptation, though Brown and Winthrop were skilful enough to avoid it. Villainy continues unabated after the Civil War in the cheaper type of fiction, but not in the work of novelists who were trying to achieve permanent literary quality. With writers like Rebecca Harding Davis, Ellen Olney Kirk, Edgar Fawcett, F. Marion Crawford, Robert Grant, Henry James, and William Dean Howells, villainy became greatly softened in tone or disappeared altogether. Our most successful painters of the city scene in the novel turned to broad canvasses—to panoramas of the social lives of their people, or to histories of their struggles to win success in the city as young artists, poets, novelists, lawyers, doctors, or business men. Satire and criticism are abundant, but exaggeration of emotions and insistence upon sensation disappear. To a large extent the realistic method prevails in dealing with city life, and the idealism which classifies all men as either saints or demons is no longer popular except in that lurid type of fiction which could not exist without it.

As one glances back at the disasters of the city as reported by our novelists, one is impressed by the absence of many outpourings of real literature. In explanation of this, one has but to note the methods with which those disasters were handled by the writers— their insistence upon dealing with duelling and intemperance as propaganda; their constant over-heightening of the emotions in dealing with poverty and villainy; and their over-indulgence in horror and terror as effects in dealing with city plagues.

The last is the most easily pardoned because the writers were only guilty of reporting too faithfully what was recognized by them as one of the greatest dangers that American cities at that time had to contend with. Because they did not understand the origin of the plagues nor the remedies for them, they became a great mystery which filled them with dread and terror, and could not have been kept out of their fiction any more readily than the disasters of the last great war could have been kept out of the contemporary fiction. Therefore, Brockden Brown and the others who wrote of yellow fever in the large cities were not conscious of reverting to the terror type of writing, but were only intent upon reporting what they knew from unpleasant personal experience.

Those novelists who joined the campaign against duelling in city and nation were working in a worthy cause and exercised potent influence in that institution's final disappearance from American life. Their efforts did not create great fiction, but they did help to arouse a dormant public opinion to a point where it could begin to see the absurdities of the code of honor.

Professional temperance writers were likewise writing for a purpose. The city appealed to them as offering them the greatest number of instances of disaster caused by drink, but their novels describing such situations became crowded with sentiment and statistics. Today they are worthless even as propaganda, so much has a spohisticated reading public outgrown the style of fiction of the T. S. Arthur type. The more skilled novelists in touching upon the problems of liquor indulgence were somewhat divided in their opinions. Several like H. C. Bunner and P. L. Ford defended the city saloon in an entertaining way by picturing graphically the important part it played in the lives of the poorer classes. Others were conscientious in denunciation of intemperate living. Fawcett became almost fanatical in opposing it and descended to school-of-terror methods in dealing with the extreme form of intoxication—delirium tremens—and in this respect he almost emulated Arthur himself. Bayard Taylor and Marion Crawford, on the other hand, treated intemperance in the only way it can be treated acceptably, namely, as a temptation to which all dwellers in the city are subject. Some of them are strong enough to triumph over it, while others through weakness are driven by it into the depths of ruin.

Horror, terror, and disgust are the emotions which our novelists strove to arouse in the readers' minds when they pictured poverty and villainy in the city. These two topics inspired more than their share of melodramatic situations, which in the case of Lippard and Miller, took the form of intense hatred towards the rich and enshrinement of the poor. It is unfortunate that the combination of supreme talent and humanitarian interest possessed so admirably by Charles Dickens was not present among any of the American city novelists who treated of the life of the poor. The Dickens influence can be seen, but those who receive it are not capable of worthy imitation of their master. Villainy, strangely enough, lies at the foundation of several of the best character creations to be found in all the novels of this "disaster group". These are Welbeck in *Arthur Mervyn* and Densdeth in *Cecil Dreme*. These men have qualities which make them real human beings whom one could imagine as actually pursuing their nefarious careers in any one of our large cities. The same praise cannot be extended to any of the villains drawn by the other novelists of the group: Fay, Irving, or Lippard.

CHAPTER III

The Religious Life of the City

Only a few contemporary novels of the period concern themselves at any great length with the religious scene as found in our large eastern cities. In a large number, on the other hand, may be found brief sketches of such life—sketches which though unimportant in relation to the whole story, yet help to reveal accurately the religious tendencies of the times.

The early American novel was negligent in attention to contemporary religious life, but by 1830 an emphasis could be noted upon conversions and revival meetings in the large cities. This phase of religion was a prominent feature of city novels written between 1830 and 1870, but from that point to the close of the century it is difficult to show any concurrence of religious emphasis. Some novels seem aware of the failure of the churches to accommodate themselves to the growing industrialism and the consequent rapid increase in urban population. The clergymen introduced in these works are often insincere, shallow, and worldly-minded; and the laymen often secure prominent places in the Church by reason of generous gifts. Some authors describe new sects as they arise, but these seem to aid very little in the city's religious problems. A few note the existence of mission churches in the slum districts. Finally, pictures are offered in several novels of that broader type of city church which interests itself in the welfare of the whole man, not only in his spiritual salvation, but his social, physical, and material development as well. This is the so-called "institutional church"* which originated in the eighties but did not reach its highest efficiency until the twentieth century. It was a definite attempt to meet the changing conditions in the large city.

The first noteworthy account of a religious service in these novels brings to attention a Methodist chapel in John Street, New York, in the early eighteen twenties. Here there is no attempt

---

*Strong, Josiah—"Religious Movements for Social Betterment", New York, 1900, 42.

to reach the whole man, but it is with the salvation of his soul that the evangelist is concerned. Further than that the chapel does not attempt to go. The novel is Miss Sedgwick's *Clarence* (1830). In it is found the casual visit of Gerald Roscoe and Gertrude Clarence to the chapel to hear Summerfield, a young English preacher whose eloquence had become widely known throughout New York. Gathered there were throngs of people of all classes. Gertrude, forced to sit apart from her escort, was not greatly interested in Summerfield's vivid description of the last judgment, the details of which the author wisely refrained from revealing to her readers. But by her side, the capricious Mrs. Layton appeared remarkably affected, so much so that tears "fell like rain-drops into her lap." Temporarily she was swept out of her usual nonchalance, but the author informs the reader that this was not a permanent condition and that soon she was her former heedless self. The inclusion of this incident was necessary to make a complete picture of the New York life of the time, for religion was an important factor in that life. The revivals there were, of course, not so robust and thrilling as rural camp-meetings, but now and then sophisticated town-folk went into ecstasies almost as violent as those habitually indulged in by the more impressionable country-folk.

Another picture of one of these meetings at the John Street Chapel shows closer approximation to the thrills of the camp-meeting. This is the one included by George W. Curtis in his *Trumps* (1859-60). Looking back thirty years or more, Curtis re-creates an astonishing spectacle of staid, dignified citizens acknowledging their deliverance from sin by rising with clasped hands and crying out loud hallelujahs. The preacher, curiously, is the same Summerfield who appeared in Miss Sedgwick's novel, but through the lapse of years he seems to have acquired greater powers of arousing emotion. Or is it that Curtis is deliberately endowing the meetings of the remote eighteen twenties with the wilder enthusiasms which did not come until the great revivals of the late fifties?

In the years 1857-8 the revival spirit reached its climax in the eastern cities. John Neal, always possessed of a superabundance of energy, from youth onward, was in his later years imbued with this religious zeal. His novel, *True Womanhood* (1859) reflects this, for though he expressly denies that it is a religious novel, the fact remains that one may find there an unrivalled record of the contemporary religious life of New York city. He portrays vividly and with an eye to the picturesque all the interesting details connected with the laymen's prayer meetings held in city churches and theatres at all hours of the day and every day in the week. He notes too that passengers on ferry boats crossing from New York to Long Island conversed more about revivals and extraordinary conversions than they did about business or stocks, or the latest reports from Europe.

Not only is there a religious background to the story, but the characters too are motivated by religious impulses. The actions of one of them seem to the modern reader incredible. Satire may have been intended by the ever-caustic Neal, when he makes the notorious Charles Parry, warm ally of thieves and gamblers, carry on an extended discussion with his sister regarding hypocrisy in Christianity. The proceeding becomes all the more absurd when it is noted that the police are in close pursuit of Charles, and thus every moment that prolongs the conference brings closer a much more serious argument in which theology will be of little assistance. In extenuation of Charles' actions it should be remembered that he had promised his mother to read one chapter in the Bible and offer one prayer every day, which promise he faithfully kept despite all his criminal associations. After conversion, Charles becomes a changed man whom his sweetheart Edith is proud to marry, though previously she had refused him on account of his lack of faith. The Byronic Arthur Maynard was guilty of skepticism in religious matters, and was endowed with a fiendish ingenuity in debate which was extremely annoying to his companions. At one of the public meetings he is made the subject of special prayer; and he too soon sees the error of his ways, and perhaps to punish him for his former irreverence, Neal has him vow a determination to study for the ministry or the foreign missionary field.

Religion entered vitally into business life, according to Kimball's *Revelations of Wall Street*. Parkinson, bankrupt after the panic of 1857, punishes Goulding, a stubborn creditor, by a rather original method. At a prayer-meeting held in a city church soon after Goulding's refusal to concur in an agreement with other creditors for the settlement of Parkinson's debts, the latter takes a seat in a front pew beside his enemy and begins to glare at him with most unchristian-like contempt. The continuance of this so disturbs Goulding that when called upon to make a public prayer, his usually glib tongue fails him, and he utters the remarkable exhortation that "Satan might *continue* to have dominion over us" and "that we all might have our portion in the lake which burneth with everlasting fire!"

Other religious touches present Parkinson in a less vengeful mood. The death of his wife and the loss of his money sobered him, but for a long time he hesitated over the complete surrender of his former unbelief. Finally, after a week of severe troubles, including arrest for implication in an alleged fraud, he seeks consolation at a church service. There he hears a sermon that at once removes his discouragement and makes him again "a happy, cheerful man."

Acquisition by individuals of the true religious spirit seems to be the controlling force behind the religious incidents just recorded. Within the years covered by these novels, eastern cities passed through several waves of religious frenzy. The one of the years 1857-8 was the most notable and the one which inspired the most significant religious reactions from our novelists, namely, those found in *True Womanhood*. Neal's work is the only sustained record of revivalism in the city, but there were others that showed a direct influence from it, such as *Trumps* and *Revelations of Wall Street*.*

After 1869 revivalism seems to have ceased to appear in our contemporary novels of city life. The great evangelistic meetings of the seventies under the leadership of Moody and Sankey had a marked effect upon the spiritual life of the people in the large cities, but inspired no important response from the novelists. Perhaps this may be explained by the fact that Moody continued his campaigns until almost the close of our period, for novelists

---

*Less important suggestions of religious conversion as found in the city may be found in Theodore Fay's *Hoboken* (1843); Mrs. Mowatt's *The Fortune Hunter* (1842); and Maria S. Cummins's *The Lamplighter* (1854).

are very reluctant to write about living persons, and certainly these meetings could not have been adequately represented in fiction without bringing in the personalities of their two great leaders. Then again, our novelists may have recognized by that time that the religious emotionalism of such meetings was not a favorable subject for fictional treatment. Religion as a subject for fiction needs an attraction that will make it universal, so that it may appeal to readers gathered from widely-variant forms of belief.

Dissatisfaction with the Church and its leaders occasionally arouses the bitter satire of our novelists. To judge from George Lippard, one would conclude that all city ministers of religion were impostors. But one cannot accept his conclusions on account of his very pronounced bias. In his treatment of the clergy in *The Quaker City* he offends against both justice and good taste. The Rev. F. Altamont T. Pyne in that novel is the founder of a religious sect which met in rowdy fashion in the upper floor of a dilapidated building in one of Philadelphia's obscure alleys. The society was probably in sympathy with the Native American movement of the 'forties, for its announced purpose is the conversion of the Pope of Rome and the suppression of Vatican Paganism. Lippard's disapproval of the efforts of the churches of his time is implied in the speech of an old man, son of a veteran of the American Revolution, who declares, greatly to the anger of Pyne's disciples, that the organization should cease directing its activities against Roman Catholicism and instead devote all its attention to missionary work in its own city, and the improvement of its courts, churches, streets, and homes. Lippard's criticism of the clergy is implied in the actions of Pyne himself, whom he represents as hastening away from the meeting to Philadelphia's worst den of vice and mystery, Monk Hall. There, safe from prying eyes, in the very centre of the city's secret life, he can spend the money which he has obtained from his disciples under the plea of appropriating it to the relief of the needy. Worse deeds also are ascribed to him.*

---

*Other slanders by Lippard against churchmen may be found in both *The Quaker City* and *The Empire City*. In the latter appears the merchant prince Evylyn Somers, who, though one of the most honored members of

More specific and more restrained satire of the Church—in this case the Episcopalian—appears in Kimball's *Was He Successful?* Rev. Augustus Myrtle, rector of St. Jude's Church in New York, is always anxious to have a spirited competition at the annual auction of rented pews. One of them is disposed of to Hiram Meeker for $1650. This unusually high price astonishes Meeker until he is told that he will sit immediately in front of the pew belonging to the rich, beautiful, and socially prominent Arabella Thorne. An opportunity is thus provided of which the ambitious Hiram makes good use, and it is not long before the church-made alliance has been completed, and Hiram is able to take possession of his bride's securities valued at more than $250,000.

In St. Jude's membership is confined almost entirely to wealthy and well-established families. Its rector preserves its exclusiveness by his studied avoidance of all contact with the poor and with all persons who are not in "the very best society." Kimball described in *To-Day* (1869) a similar Episcopal church as being "the most fashionably select church in New York."* The Rev. Croton Ellsworth, its rector, is insincere but popular, and although he figures discreditably in a celebrated will case, this does not affect his standing with his congregation.

With the novels of Mrs. H. B. Stowe, especially *My Wife and I* (1871) and *We and Our Neighbors* (1873), the reader has opened before him the whole problem of the Church's treatment of the poor, the friendless, and the unfortunate in the large city. In her mind the Church was doing a much more effective work than it was reported to be doing in the novels of Lippard and Kimball. Her attitude towards it is enthusiastic, though she is perfectly aware of the existence of superficialities in religious emphasis as found in churches catering to the so-called aristocratic classes. Her young hero, Harry Henderson, finds at once a congenial and sociable church where the congregation is composed largely of young men who like himself are strangers in New York, away

---

Trinity Church, has been guilty in commercial life of unscrupulous practices by which he has robbed hundreds of their homes.

*This association of fashion and religion is noticed by Howells thirteen years later in *A Modern Instance,* when he has Marcia Hubbard choose the church "where the best people go."

from home and friends. She declares that Henderson there met types of some of "those good old-fashioned Christians that Hawthorne celebrates in his 'Celestial Railroad' under the name of Messrs. 'Stick to the Right' and 'Foot it to Heaven', men better known among the poor and afflicted than in fashionable or literary circles, men . . . . who are footing it to heaven on the old time-worn, narrow way, and carrying with them as many as they can induce to go."*

After marriage, Henderson and his wife Eva attend a small Episcopal mission church which is convenient to their home. Eva's Aunt Maria is greatly disturbed that she has left her conservative Episcopal church with its amiable middle-aged rector, devoted to "our excellent liturgy and from his heart opposed to anything which made trouble."† She protests against Eva's joining a church which had as leader a High Churchman like the young missionary St. John, who belonged to the modern Anglican wing of the English Church. But as a matter of fact, St. John's church practices came nearer to meeting the changing conditions of modern city life than did those of the hide-bound rector of Aunt Maria's church. For example, St. John had established a mission for the poor and had sponsored the Refuge of the Sisters of St. Barnabas. The latter was a receiving station for homeless and desolate people, where they could find temporary shelter.

A visit to the slums of New York is described by Mrs. Stowe. There the Hendersons are taken through a Methodist mission that carries out an extensive program for the benefit of homeless wanderers gathered in by its superintendent. The building contains a sitting-room, work-room with several sewing-machines and a kitchen where soup is served every night. An enlargement is planned for the mission so as to put in dormitories for men who are willing to take the pledge to abandon drinking; there it is hoped that they can find shelter until some kind of employment can

---

*Stowe, Harriet B.—"My Wife and I", Boston and New York (1871), Riverside Edition, 135-6.
†Suggestion of a similar "hands-off" policy from the pulpit is provided in the satiric portrait drawn by William H. Bishop in *The House of the Merchant Prince* (1883) of the pastor of a large Fifth Avenue church, the polished Dr. Miltimore. He is represented as softening the asperities of theology, never touching on politics, or even religion, and thus offending the susceptibilities of no man.

be provided for them. Here then is the Church actively engaged in social work—a far cry from the exclusive or fashionable church depicted by Kimball, and from the evangelical institution depicted by Miss Sedgwick, Curtis, and Neal.

A Quaker* woman preacher is portrayed as being remarkable for her dignity and confidence in her own abilities. She is able through the quiet impressiveness of her character to go through the slums, at midnight and alone, and to speak words to bar-tenders and keepers of brothels, which if a man had uttered them, would have cost him his life.

A smaller segment of the religious life of the city is presented in Howells' *The Undiscovered Country*. Written in 1880, this novel surveys conditions of some years before, probably at least twenty, when spiritualism was comparatively new. A country doctor's attempt to practice the occult in Boston, using his daughter Egeria as medium, proves a pathetic failure, because his own faith in spiritualism will not permit an alliance with chicanery. The reader is introduced to a street in the city whose houses are inhabited mostly by fortune-tellers and charlatans of low degree. At Mrs. Le Roy's séance there is a small group of enthusiasts carefully delineated. There is Mr. Eccles, a fussy, precise inquirer; Mr. Hatch, smartly-dressed and genial, whose good-humor is greatly at variance with the sobriety of all the others; and among the women is one who is very emotional—almost hysterical. The séance proceeds in the usual way, and ends in a manner very gratifying to Dr. Boynton, but the next day he learns that he has been duped. While he regards spiritualism as a religion with which is bound up his hope of immortality, Mrs. Le Roy, a medium lately come from the West, cares for it only in so far as it has brought her in some easy money. She is on a par with the other charlatans on the same street. Dr. Boynton concludes that the city is not the proper sphere for the operation of his spiritualistic experiments. He finds that the Bostonians who came

---

*The Gilded Age, written in the same year (1873), contains another interesting Quaker character in Ruth Bolton, a young girl who is dissatisfied with the severities of Friendly doctrines, rarely attends the Philadelphia meeting, and is permitted to leave the Quaker academy at Westfield, which she designates as "a place to turn young people into dried fruit." Eventually she studies medicine.

to his public exhibitions for the first time are often quite frank to express their enthusiasm and to ask for the privilege of pursuing investigations with Egeria as medium. But they rarely take advantage of the cordial invitation to call, and indeed rarely return for a second séance. In other words, they have looked upon Dr. Boynton as a new city sensation into which they must investigate because their friends have done so, but once they have paid their visit, they quickly pass to another sensation. Since the city people are so indifferent, the doctor thinks that it would be better for him to resume his former efforts with rural followers, few in number, but purely disinterested. Later experiences take him into a Shaker community where spiritualism is taught as a means and not an end. Here he finally comes to understand that spiritualism, on the whole, is notably deficient as a rule of life. Howells' novel is far more significant artistically than the others considered so far in this section, because its characters are more carefully and realistically depicted and its scenes are more sharply and accurately sketched. The author does not pretend that spiritualism could solve the religious problems of city life. He shows its limited scope.* Even the enthusiastic Dr. Boynton sees in it only a possible link between inhabitants of this world and those of the other world who have gone before them.

The desire of individuals whose lives are controlled by religious motives to have the lives of their friends or lovers similarly controlled is not unusual in city life especially when, as in Neal's *True Womanhood,* the city is passing through a period of religious revival. In 1884, Robert Grant presented in *An Average Man* another such situation, but without any connection with revivalism. Two young people are there shown attracted to each other because they are both intensely interested in the spiritual side of life. They are members of families of good social standing but have little money. The girl, Dorothy Crosby, was troubled by thoughts of the futility of the daily rounds of balls, dinner parties, and the other entertainments of the city, which, though she en-

---

*Mrs. Rebecca H. Davis offers a picture of a spiritualistic séance in *A Law Unto Herself* (1878) in an abandoned, gray stone house in one of the suburbs of Philadelphia. The medium for the occasion is exposed as an absolute fraud, much to the disgust of the learned investigators assembled, and the séance terminates in confusion.

joyed, seemed to her to lead nowhere. Her conviction that there
was a divine purpose in life was shared by Arthur Remington, a
young lawyer. When they became engaged, he told her that "for
you and me there can be no rest or happiness save in striving to
conquer evil." Their participation in church work is not mentioned, but Dorothy's individual efforts are seen in the persuasive
words which she uses to convince her friend, Mrs. Stoughton, that
divorce is not compatible with Christian teaching. She and her
husband thus represent Grant's emphasis on the religious life of
the city as seen from the point of view of the individual rather
than from that of the Church.

In *The Yoke of the Thorah* (1887) Henry Harland (Sidney
Luska) presents a common problem of crowded life as it is found
in large cities, namely, intermarriage between persons of widely-
variant religious sects. Here it is proposed marriage between a
Jewish artist and a Christian girl. The rabbi uncle prevents the
contemplated union, but the result is a tragic one for the artist.
Harland's thesis is that marriage between two young people
deeply and sincerely in love should not be stopped because of discrepancies in religion. Unfortunately, his thinly-disguised propaganda advocating this mars the attractiveness of an otherwise
charming picture of the manners and customs of orthodox Jews
in the New York of the eighties.

Grandison Mather (1889), by the same author, does not stress
the problem of intermarriage to any appreciable extent. The
religious elements centre about Mr. Grickel, an elderly German
Jew who lectures on Sunday evenings in a New York public hall
before the Society for Humane Culture.* This organization was
founded by Grickel primarily for liberal Jews, but membership
was not denied to Christians. The founder, himself a Jew, believes that Christ was the greatest of the prophets and that men
should observe his teachings literally. He had a broad conception
of the duties of a religious body and was thus in agreement with
the liberal churchmen of the time. The socialized activities of
the Society include a training school for nurses, an industrial

---

*This name at once suggests the Society for Ethical Culture, organized
in New York in 1876 by Felix Adler. Like Grickel's society, Ethical
Culture drew its membership from both Jew and Gentile.

school for poor children where they may learn the English language and also a trade, and a Relief Fund devoted to the needs of the poor. Therefore, it stands as an illustration of a religious organization striving to meet the challenge presented to it by the trying conditions of a large cosmopolitan community.

The most extended and most sympathetic treatment of a city minister thus far met with in this review* is that found in Howells' *The Minister's Charge* (1886). This novel presents the difficulties in the life of a city pastor in an unique manner, for the author does not dwell upon the variety and multiplicity of his parish duties, but concentrates his attention upon his relations with one individual. Lemuel Barker, rustic, arrives unexpectedly at Mr. Sewell's door, but the latter is primarily responsible for the young man's migration to the city with, figuratively speaking, a sheaf of poems in each hand. Sewell follows closely Barker's progress, discourages him firmly from further pursuit of an unsympathetic Muse, and aids from time to time by securing him a better position, or by fatherly advice, which if it had fallen upon heeding ears, would have prevented a great deal of trouble. Lemuel's mild successes in the city develop him into an enthusiastic upholder of its advantages over those of the country. His rusticity becomes less marked, and he is rapidly being converted into an useful, though humble citizen. Quickly he passes from furnace-tender to elevator-boy, then to head-waiter who will not take tips, then to hotel clerk, and finally, reader to a gentleman of leisure and refinement. His own self-improvement is not neglected, for he is regular in attendance at church, particularly Sewell's, and goes to all the learned lectures that Boston provides in such abundance. In everything Sewell seems to be his ideal, but in two crises he fails him. When Barker calls on the first of these occasions, it is the minister's vacation period, and it is only by chance that he is at home. As it happens, he is in Boston over night, on his way to be the "supply" in a friend's pulpit at New Bedford. He apologizes that he is engaged in scrambling together

---

*Mrs. Elizabeth (Stuart) Phelps' *A Peep at "Number Five" or A Chapter in the Life of a City Pastor* (1852) should not be wholly disregarded, for it gives an adequate, if somewhat placid, representation of the problems of a city minister in the Boston of the 1850's. The plot is negligible.

a sermon, asks Barker a few questions about his work and his health, but gives him little encouragement to introduce the vital problem which has brought him to the parsonage. Lemuel understands at once that Sewell wants him to go, even in spite of his polite query. "Is there anything—something—you wished to speak with me about?" His decision, he realizes, must be made independently of the minister's help. Naturally, his inexperience leads him to make the wrong one.

Barker's next visit to Sewell finds him again engrossed in composition. He and his wife have just returned from a long vacation. Neither church nor parsonage has yet resumed its regular routine. Visitors, especially a difficult one like Lemuel, are not entirely welcome. Mrs. Sewell, always jealous of unnecessary interruptions to her husband while he is writing his sermons, persuades him that it would be better for her to see Barker. She talks with him for a few minutes in a not very cordial manner, and then Barker leaves without broaching at all his problem—the most vital of all that he has had to face in his city career. He has decided the next day to remain loyal to the shop-girl, Statira Dudley, who with her grave deficiencies of education and breeding, and her chronic attacks of serious illness, can never be anything but a drawback to his progress. Pity for her has greatly influenced his decision. In thus choosing Statira, he has abandoned all hope of winning a young woman more refined and more suitable for him in every way who has come to love him. She it is who would undoubtedly have been Sewell's choice if Barker had been allowed to explain the situation to him. As it is, she goes out of Barker's life completely, and he lowers himself to the standards of Statira, and eventually has to leave the city and return to the country to take work as teacher in a rural school.

Howells is relentless in showing Sewell's responsibiilty for Barker's failure to remain in the city; but, of course, some of the blame must be ascribed to Barker's own nature which was ill adapted to withstand the trials of city life; and some of the blame must be borne by Mrs. Sewell for her open disapproval of him to her husband, who like many ministers, valued his wife's opinion far above its actual worth. The experiences with Barker provided Sewell with themes for several sermons. One of these contained the doctrine of complicity which, when expounded from the pulpit made a deep impression, for it was peculiarly applicable to city conditions, where men's lives are so inextricably involved one with the other. Briefly, it declares that no one stands apart from his fellows, but each is bound to the highest and lowest by ties that centre in the hand of God.*

It is only a short step from Sewell's complicity teaching to that abiding concern for the welfare of her fellow creatures which was possessed by the heroine of *The Faith Doctor,* written by Edward Eggleston in 1891. Phillida Callender, daughter of a foreign missionary who died after a return to this country, becomes attracted into healing work through a sincere belief in the efficacy of faith as announced in the Scriptures. She is enabled to accomplish a series of remarkable "cures" among the poor of New York city, with whom she comes into contact by her work in a mission Sunday-school. Remarkable as these seem to be, they do not cause Phillida to over-estimate her powers. She will not allow herself to be classed with professional faith-healers, and will not be dragged into a commercial alliance with a Christian Science practitioner who promises her large returns if she will aid her in gaining an entrée into the more influential and wealthy homes of the city. Phillida's success comes only in cases where the afflicted person's will needs to be aroused. Far from being a fraud, as the officious practitioner Miss Bowyer is declared to be, she will not take cases which show signs of being germ-carried diseases. Indeed her attitude towards healing is at small variance with that of the medical profession. The author is obviously trying to excuse a mild form of faith-healing when he has a medical doctor say to Phillida that the new faith-cure people enlist the will in their cures and "they often help chronic invalids whom the doctors have failed to benefit."†

Christian Science as far as it was concerned with faith-healing among the less enlightened classes of New York City, is presented in a very unfavorable light in this novel. Miss Bowyer's attempts to cure the young Martin boy stricken with diphtheria are satirized and made to appear ludicrous. They have no soothing effect

---

*Howells, William D.—"The Minister's Charge", Boston, 1887, 409.
†Eggleston, Edward—"The Faith Doctor", New York, 1891, 394.

upon the sick child, who "kicked and cried in a way which showed him to be utterly out of harmony with the odylic emanations of the terrestrial magnet."* This lack of harmony was one of the symptoms that the practitioner was probably trying to remedy without success. Her efforts soon ceased, however, for the rich cousin of Mrs. Martin threatened to report her to the County Medical Society and the Board of Health for practicing her art on a contagious disease, contrary to law."† The religious interest of the story lies, as has already been implied, in Phillida Callender's strong belief in Christian faith as a remedy for many of man's ills of a physical nature, especially those which can be traced to a deficiency in will power and super-abundance of imagination.

Earnestness in religious matters may become so intense as to cross that narrow border line separating religious devotion from insanity. This often happens to persons living in our large cities, where obsession by a religious mania is altogether too common. Howells paints such a person in Denton *(The World of Chance.)* In his case, the obsession is the notion that sin is to be atoned for by some kind of sacrifice or expiation. He has invented a new process which promised to bring him a great deal of money but, overpowered by the thought that it will take work away from hundreds of persons, he destroys it just before it is completed. When his twin daughters die from scarlet fever, he believes that God has taken them from him to atone for his sin. Shelley Ray finds him one Sunday sitting in the Park on a bench with head bent down, apparently oblivious to all his surroundings. Frequently he will stop in his conversations to listen to a Voice which he thinks he hears and which governs his every action. His father-in-law, the venerable Hughes, veteran of the Brook Farm and other community experiments, explains to Ray that the Voice is probably a survival of some of Denton's supernatural experiences among the Shakers, who reared him. Ray aptly character-

---

*ibid., p. 357.

†It is interesting to note that only eleven years after the publication of *The Faith Doctor*, Mrs. Mary Baker Eddy advised the public that "until public thought becomes better acquainted with Christian Science, the Christian Scientists shall decline to doctor infectious or contagious diseases." . . . See Harold U. Faulkner, "The Quest for Social Justice, 1898-1914", New York, 1931, 214.

izes him as a "crank". Denton's last obsession is that the Voice desires him to sacrifice the best, purest, meekest person in New York. To him this can be none other than his sister-in-law, Peace Hughes, the girl who, alone of his family, is able to control him when he is in one of his spells. Therefore, he tries to kill Peace by making her swallow prussic acid, but is prevented by the combined efforts of Ray and Hughes. He breaks away from them, enters his room, and takes the acid himself. While religion is the immediate cause of his mania, it is the opinion of Hughes and others that the city environment has increased an eccentricity that already existed while he was living outside of the city. Thus Hughes said a few weeks before Denton's death that "the hard experiences of the city have not been good for him. . . . It would be well if he could be got into the country somewhere."* Ray reports after Denton's death, to Mr. Brandreth, the publisher, that "the doctor says nothing would have happened . . . . if the man had stayed quietly in the country, in the routine he was used to. But when he had the stress of new circumstances put on him, with the anxieties and the chances, and all the miseries around him, his mind gave way."† Brandreth was concerned lest if undue publicity should be given to Denton's suicide, his name would be dragged into the papers through Peace Hughes, who is his secretary. But Howells ironically explains that the suicide "was treated as one of those every-day tragedies without significance or importance . . . . which abound in the history of great cities, and are forgotten as rapidly as they occur."‡

From Brander Matthews, a great admirer of Howells, one may obtain in *His Father's Son*, some hints of big business in the Church. They seem authentic, coming as they do from a man who was himself the son of a wealthy father and could mingle without question among New York's rich men and noted celebrities. The congregation at the church where Ezra Pierce, millionaire business man, attends is said by statistical reporters to represent a capital of at least one hundred million dollars. When the minister, Dr. Thurston, preaches one Sunday evening against

---

*Howells, William D.—"The World of Chance", New York, 1893, 245.
†ibid., 278.
‡ibid., 288.

the rich, Pierce's daughter-in-law, listening, is not quite certain that his words ring true. Others, no doubt, among the audience felt the same way. Ezra, Puritanical in his regulations regarding the Sabbath routine in his home, is not above desecrating it himself by staying home Sunday evenings to talk over financial affairs with his broker. Finances are Ezra's passion, so that it is natural that even in church life it should be the financial aspect of it that claims his attention. Dr. Thurston always finds him generous. For example, one evening when he comes to Pierce with a plan for relief of the poor, Ezra is willing to pledge $10,000 or even $15,000 of the needed $100,000 on condition that the remainder is raised by the other members of the church.* Dr. Thurston is grateful, but that same evening he is not a little embarrassed when Winslow Pierce comes home, visibly and vocally intoxicated. The scene is quite awkward, but no doubt a recollection of the father's generous gift causes the good man to relax a little of his severity towards the erring son. A pastor of a church that caters to Wall Street cannot be too scrupulous about the vices of the sons of Wall Street. Dr. Thurston is depicted more capably and more realistically than the other pastors of large, fashionable churches whom we have met in the novels of Kimball and Bishop. None, however, is made more than a minor character.

Leaving New York temporarily, we enter with Arlo Bates, novelist and college professor of English, into the polite circles of Boston in the closing years of the century. The quick-changing sketches which *The Puritans* (1898) gives of the artificiality of religion as found among the idle rich of that city are satirical, but there is no doubt that they present, on the whole, a truthful picture. In its endeavor to cover a broad slice of city life, the novel jumps rapidly from one fad of society to another, omitting few that were of importance at the time. Those that are particularly urban in character group themselves under the general heading of "heresies and strange doctrines." Some of these are already

---

*It can be imagined that Thomas Mavick (Warner's *That Fortune*) exerted just as much power financially in St. Agnes's Church. Warner declares satirically that the fact that Mavick and his family "worshipped regularly at St. Agnes's was a guarantee of the stability of that Church, and incidentally marked the success of the Christian religion in the metropolis." (pp. 70-71).

familiar, but a few are met here for the first time. All reflect closely contemporary religious fashions. They are exhibited at social gatherings in Boston's most exclusive homes, held mostly in the afternoons. Men are scarce there. The two young novices, Philip Ashe and Maurice Wynne, are privileged to attend because their clergy house has been recently damaged by fire so that they have had to take shelter in private homes. One of the newest crazes which their hostesses show these young men is that for the mystical philosophy and religion of the East. Thus a Persian is represented as entertaining Boston women with his entrancing readings of his country's cycle of mystic hymns. His explanations arouse the anger of Philip Ashe; and his vigorous protest inaugurates a general discussion. Ashe notes with dismay the shallow reasoning of the women and their general acceptance of the tradition that speakers on such occasions could appear profoundly serious but "it would not do to be really in earnest." A spiritualistic séance conducted by an amateur is vividly described and, as usual, ends with exposure of the medium. Faith-healing also claimed a share of attention. A lecture upon this subject by a practitioner of "Christian Faith Healed" provides Bates with an excellent opportunity for use of his keen satire on the shallowness of Boston women's interest in such affairs. As soon as the lecturer has completed her vehement denial of the existence of death and has risen from her chair signifying the close of her discourse, the women at once resume their former life, just as if nothing had happened. Immediately is heard "the exchange of greetings and bits of news, the making of appointments for shopping or theatre-going, and all the trivial chat of daily life."* Religion, Bates would have the reader believe, was a kind of pastime with Bostonians of that time. His epigram expresses the situation aptly: "In Boston there are many persons whose chief object in life seems to be the discovery of novel forms of spiritual dissipation."†

Miss Ellen Glasgow, writing in the same year as Arlo Bates, contributed in her *Phases of an Inferior Planet* to the religious scene in the city with a study of an Episcopalian minister,

---

*Bates, Arlo—"The Puritans", Boston and New York, 1898, 72.
†ibid., p. 5.

Anthony Algarcife, who was tempted to abandon his church and devote himself to worldly matters. His final decision to remain faithful to his sacred calling was influenced greatly by realization of the vast amount of practical good which his church was accomplishing in the city of New York through its many and varied activities. The Church of the Immaculate Conception, of which he was rector, is an excellent illustration of an institutional church. Algarcife's arduous duties, in connection with it, call upon him to preach regularly to his own rich Fifth Avenue congregation; to attend to all their spiritual needs; to teach hygiene at his Bowery mission; and to give Sunday night lectures on the care of children. His interests are evenly divided between Fifth Avenue and East Side. The fact that with all his seeming enthusiasm he is at heart a religious sceptic, makes his success all the more striking, even if somewhat improbable. At the end, when he contemplates leaving the church and his position there, more is learned of the broad scope of his work. While sitting in his study, he is kept busy attending to the calls from his people. Thus, a man from the Bowery, just released after a year in jail, comes to consult him on how to go straight; an assistant brings in the name of a child who is to be received into the Orphanage. Another summons shows the close connection of his church with the city's industrial life, for he is informed that some of his men at the Beasly Rolling Mills have gone on strike and have used violence. His presence is needed at once to prevent further bloodshed. This proves to be the one thing needed to make him see the impossibility of his leaving the church without incurring the everlasting reproach of all those who now believe in him. This novel, while not so significant in the light of Miss Glasgow's later works, is valuable today, if for nothing else, in its revelation that by 1898 the social program of the large city church was in active operation. Judging from the casual, unsensational way in which Algarcife's church is described, we may safely presume that other city churches were engaged in smiliar programs.

In recapitulation, it may be stated that a fairly comprehensive survey of the urban religious life in this period may be obtained from reading the few city novels which are primarily religious in nature and supplementing them by the perusal of religious episodes selected from novels covering other phases of city life. The episodes are instructive in themselves but have little connection, as a rule, with the plot.

The novels that show extended representation of religious life in the cities are not all of the first rank from the standpoint of characterization and plot. Neal's *True Womanhood* is an instance of this, for it contains no life-like portraits and, as usual with Neal, the story is confused and disjointed. An accurate portrayal of the religious revivals of the time provides it with its only possible claim to permanence.

The efforts of writers like Howells, Eggleston, Arlo Bates, and Ellen Glasgow are more praiseworthy. Of two novels by Howells fundamentally religious in subject—*The Undiscovered Country* and *The Minister's Charge*—the first is significant for its account of the reception of spiritualism in the city of Boston, but the best portions of the story are generally admitted to be those that occur outside of the city in connection with the peaceful village life of the Shakers. *The Minister's Charge,* while entirely concerned with an urban religious problem, treats it from a too restricted viewpoint. Consequently, the reader misses the inclusion of those wider aspects of the religious scene which are so characteristic of urban religious organizations. To compensate for these deficiencies one may cite the vivid portraits of Sewell, his interfering wife, and the helpless Lemuel Barker. Discriminating readers also may be impressed by Howell's teaching that in the large city every man is responsible in no uncertain way for the actions of his fellow men. *The Faith Doctor,* another full-length religious picture, is marred by Eggleston's apparent unfamiliarity with the city scene, especially with its social aspects. It is true, however, that Phillida Callender has reality and arouses sympathy by her true spirituality and her sincere advocacy of faith-healing at a time when health fakers were all too numerous in the large cities. *The Puritans* is a brilliant panorama of the religious scene in a section of Boston's social life, but the author has spoiled it by his flippant attitude towards life and his absorption in the religious crazes or fads of the city to the exclusion of its more orthodox sects. In *Phases of an Inferior Planet*

is found another cynical picture but one which is ennobled somewhat at the end of the story by the apparent acquiescence of the
unbelieving rector in his task and his final realization of its
sacredness.

CHAPTER IV

THE SOCIAL LIFE OF THE CITY

The one who enters upon the study of the social life of the American city with the expectation of finding there nothing but friendliness and geniality is certain to be disappointed. Those qualities are, of course, two of the most distinctive marks of true companionship in the city or elsewhere, but unfortunately other and less desirable qualities, such as unfriendly rivalry and envy, enter very largely into the lives of city dwellers. Recognition of this fact is necessary before one can have a complete understanding of the meaning of "social life" as it is now generally used. Our novelists were probably all the more readily attracted to this phase of the city's life by reason of the mixture of friendliness and hatred. They were attracted also by the variegated strata of the urban social world and by the fact that they found there spontaneous situations admirably adapted to their art.

The compiler of this record is well aware that this social phase of the life of the city has already been stressed in a number of instances in the preceding chapters. This was unavoidable, for an individual's striving for recognition in the eyes of his fellow men often forms an important part of his success or failure in the city; and the disasters of an individual's existence cannot always be separated from social events which precede them; and even in the religious life of the city one may find connections, as in the case of the institutional church which stresses social as well as spiritual values. In the present chapter an effort has been made to avoid as far as possible repetition of situations already used. It has been thought best to concentrate on those phases that are particularly urban in their nature. These may be stated as follows: the jealous adherence by long-established families to the tradition that prestige in the city is and should be based upon good-breeding; the disapproval and positive horror with which such patrician families look upon what seems to them the unwarranted invasion of their sacred precincts by a class of people whose sesame for admission is "money"; the incessant striving of certain types of individuals in the city to outdo all others in the magnificence of their dwellings and in the brilliance and expansiveness of the entertainments given there; and the craze of American families for foreign fashions in manners, art, literature, and speech, a craze which generally took the form of Anglomania. Contrast is the one theme that the novelists found predominant in their study of social relationships of the city, and it is the progress of this theme that we shall strive to trace throughout this chapter.

In some of our earliest novels, social life is not sufficiently identified with the city to make it worthy of attention. For example, in *Arthur Mervyn* the hero soon after becoming accustomed to the city, becomes aware that there is a social side to his nature which has not yet been cultivated. He begins active pursuit of what he has missed, but his experiences are not at all different from those of any other callow youth, rural or urban, who is faced with the dilemma of choosing between a simple-minded country girl of about his own age and a woman of the world many years older. With Catherine M. Sedgwick, however, city social life is made more distinctive, and her readers realize that she presents social situations as they actually exist in the city.

A novel that is characteristic of Miss Sedgwick's work is *Clarence* (1830). Here one finds the comparative method used to good advantage, when Miss Clarence, the heiress of Clarence-ville and former resident of New York, on a return to the city visits some of her former neighbors. One family on whom she calls, the Browns, represents New York's newly rich from an unusual point of view, for they are not, as often in such cases, offensive in display of their wealth Stephen Brown, who was formerly a tailor on Chatham Street, still preserved his fondness for the tailor's trade when increased fortunes enabled him to move into a costly home on Broadway. The gaudy furnishings of the house show that acquisition of money by its owners had not helped to develop in them an artistic taste. The parlor was crowded with ill-assorted furniture, but more conspicuous than anything else was a huge chandelier, large enough to light a theatre. In the basement one found more comfort and less ornament. Here Brown was busy at a table, putting new cuffs on an old coat;

and his wife was assorting shreds and patches for a rag carpet—tasks which they undertook not through necessity but for the satisfaction to be obtained from industry, to which they had long been accustomed before attaining to their present station. Miss Clarence was cordially received by them; her true democratic spirit was revealed in her ability to enter at once into the inmost lives of these former friends, who despite their hard-earned money, were still far below the high social rating to which she herself had attained. It is one of those peaceful scenes which Miss Sedgwick could depict with impressive skill; but sentiment soon made its appearance in the guise of mourning for the Brown's wayward son, exiled from home by his father's express command.

At a morning visit described in this same novel, the author satirizes the intolerance of those who are safely within the inner gates towards those who are just outside knocking for admission. It is only one of several indictments against the artificiality and hypocrisy of fashionable life that Miss Sedgwick offers in this novel, but it is particularly significant as representing an attitude of mind which was common in novels of urban social life throughout the period. It is introduced here by means of a heated discussion among fashionable men and women whether they shall condescend to attend a tea party to which they have been invited by the Spencers. The debate is being waged on the question of the gentility of the family. Some think them "visitable"; others recall certain disqualifying features about them, such as the circumstance that Mrs. Spencer before her marriage made a living by dressmaking. The decision becomes favorable to the Spencers when "blues" like Miss Clarence and Miss Mayo throw their influence towards them. To some of the newest arrivals in the set the result is quite displeasing; the author understands, of course, that the most hide-bound and intolerant members of the city's *haut monde* in many instances were those whose claims to membership were just as insecure as those of the uneducated John Smith of this story, whose father drove a hackney coach when he first came to New York. The scene is good-humored satire; but it is clear that the author was sincere in condemnation of the shallowness of the city's social standards.

Artificiality is also seen by James Fenimore Cooper in the standards of the New York social world as he draws it in the earlier part of *Home as Found* (1838). He is well aware of the deep contrasts to be found there and has nothing but praise for the few who remain its titular heads by virtue of "position, education, manners, association, mind, fortune, and birth." One of these is Mrs. Hawker, and by implication, at least, Cooper would class with her the Effinghams who have just returned from a long European visit. Other sets, consisting mostly of those who are newcomers to New York, are not at all aware of the existence of Mrs. Hawker and of her indisputable right to leadership. They have quickly accumulated large fortunes and have indulged in vulgar and uninstructed finery so that her manners and her polished and simple mind would find little sympathy among them, for they belong to a class who "seldom rise above a commonplace sentiment without getting upon stilts."*

Cooper's sympathy was entirely with the social ideals of the older families of New York life, those who, though few in number, had been unspoiled by the influx of the levelling tendencies of Jacksonian democracy. The social climber and the *nouveau riche* aroused his contempt. One of the former is the ambitious Mrs. Jared Jarvis, wife of a sensible, painstaking business man. Her "itching desire to figure in the world of fashion" is not shared by her husband. He is perfectly willing to admit the existence of inequalities of rank among people of the city. Thus, he declares to her that he believes that Edward Effingham is a more finished gentleman than he is, and that a tacit acknowledgment of that fact will please him. Mrs. Jarvis disagrees and boldly asserts that she considers herself fit to associate with anybody in the country, to which Jarvis very wisely replies: "If you wish the world to believe you the equal of any one, no matter whom, do not be always talking about it, lest they see you distrust the fact yourself."†

Mrs. Houston, whose balls and other entertainments were always well attended, and who was personally quite popular, represented a type of leader whom Cooper ranked just a little

---

*Cooper, James Fenimore—"Home as Found", 2 v., Phila., 1838, v. 1, 62.
†ibid, v. 1, 55.

below Mrs. Hawker. She came of a family which though acceptable was "one much less elevated in the olden time" than that of the former lady's. Cooper cannot entirely permit himself to express approval of her; his satire vents itself upon the company gathered at her house—upon their noisy conversations and their absurd rules of etiquette. Some of the latter, as announced by the belle Miss Ring provide that no well-bred young lady should move about a drawing-room or dance floor without a gentleman's arm to lean on, and two ladies should not under any circumstances converse together without a gentleman being near at hand. When Eve Effingham violates the first of these regulations, Miss Ring is shocked and will not excuse her action on the ground, as a young man reminds her, that Eve is a privileged character since she is a Hajji, a person who has made the pilgrimage to Paris.

The fondness for the foreign scene and foreign fashions is presented to some slight extent in *Home as Found* in the condescension of several of the returned Americans towards New York in comparison with their recollections of European centres like Paris, Rome, or Vienna which they had recently visited. Mr. Howel, who "uses English spectacles for all he looks at," and "English opinions for all he says," is unfortunately a product of rural Templeton and cannot, therefore, be claimed for an early illustration of urban Anglomania.

Cooper's delineation of the social scene in the city is not so memorable as Miss Sedgwick's, perhaps owing to the fact that he found the frontier and the sea more attractive subjects for his art. In writing *Home as Found* he was actuated by a spirit of dissatisfaction with his countrymen; hence, the book is full of caustic criticism. The characters are wooden puppets created by him simply to utter his views with respect to social conditions in New York, a town which to use his own words, "resembles an encampment, quite as much as it resembles a permanent and a long-existing capital."*

A lighter and more good-natured tone prevails in Mrs. Anna Cora Mowatt's *The Fortune Hunter* (1842), which she describes as a "Novel of New York Society." The man-about-town,

---

*ibid., vol. 1, 55.

Augustus Brainard, whose adventures in seeking to live by his wits in New York provide the plot of the novel, is not an admirable representative of any section of society. The reader is not sympathetic with his selfish efforts to obtain a fortune by means of marriage with a rich girl. Therefore, his final discomfiture when he finds that the supposed city heiress who has accepted him is in reality as penniless as himself, is not a disappointment. From the social standpoint, Brainard is the least notable of all the characters. His is not social ambition, since he is moved principally by a desire to secure a wife who will be able to pay his debts for him. He is excelled in interest by the ubiquitous Badger, a bill collector notorious for boldness and for success in approaching his victims, bill in hand, at the most embarrassing moments possible. Badger's conversation is racy and humorous; his presence always insures a comic relief. His greatest feat was his collection of a bill from the Methodist minister by means of boldly entering the church, taking a front seat and gazing so fixedly at his victim in the pulpit that the harassed clergyman could not concentrate on his well-prepared sermon and had to stop at "firstly" instead of his customary sixthly or seventhly. His parishioners commented after the service in a puzzled manner that this was his shortest sermon on record. Needless to relate, Badger obtained his money promptly the next morning. He did not hesitate also to stop Brainard and any other young man and present bills to them while they were walking on Broadway in company with young ladies of fashion.

Brainard's determination to have a rich wife brings him into relationship with several eligible young women in and out of the city's social circles. Mrs. Mowatt shows by her treatment of these that she understood the city of her time. The Clinton sisters, Rachel and Esther, daughters of a retired hardware merchant, and possessed of potential fortunes of $100,000 each, are not members of an old Knickerborcker family, but, nevertheless, they move in the most exclusive set. This fact arouses no resentment on her part, for she believes that the best standards for admission to good society are not family tradition, but cultivated manners and upright conduct.

The old New York family does not receive the preference as it does in Cooper's novel, but it is aristocracy of wealth which obtains Mrs. Mowatt's approval. She does, however, include in her novel a representative of the former in the person of Miss Priscilla Adair, who is said to be of the Adairs that "belong to our old-fashioned New York aristocracy—a class of persons that were once in the ascendant, but have seen their best days in the *beau monde,* which has become too dreadfully mixed for their exclusiveness."*

Mrs. Mowatt's work exhibits a verve and reality in the social scenes altogether lacking in Cooper, and she excels Miss Sedgwick in one respect, at least, that is, in her male portraits. Her characters are real city people, and their conversations are amusing or edifying as may be dictated by their personalities. They are representative of types which are as well known now as they were in the 1840's: the fortune-hunter, male or female (Brainard and Priscilla Adair), the officious bill-collector (Badger), the young girl who thrives on the reading of the latest romances and weeps over the "ideal griefs of ideal beings" and has no tears left for "the real sorrows of many a poor wretch whom her bounty might have succored" (Esther Clinton), and the young woman of wealth who plans to remain single and have her own career but promptly forgets all such ideals when a young man offers her his love (Rachel Clinton).

Satire of the newly rich is resumed in *The Barclays of Boston* (1854), by Mrs. Harrison G. Otis. The Barclays themselves are safely established in one of the higher stations of Boston's polite world, but the Bartons, especially the two daughters of the family, are social climbers. They provide the author with the material for a great deal of her ridicule on account of their lack of any real accomplishments. Their father, a self-made city merchant, gave them an expensive education, but this was of no permanent benefit to them, since after it was finished, they were still not entirely proficient in any one thing, but "drew a little, played a little, and sang a vast deal, with remarkably unmusical voices, and

---

*Mowatt, Mrs. Anna C. (Helen Berkley)—"The Fortune Hunter" (1842) edition of 1844, New York, p. 23.

talked immensely of all the 'ologies, to which were superadded chemistry and medicine."*

The elaborate dinner given by the Bartons is a clever caricature of the lower order of Boston society to which they have gained admission. Barton was annoyed that the dinner courses were announced in French, since, as he knew nothing of that polite language, he could not, as a generous host should, offer his guests any second helpings. Humor is obtained too, by the circumstance that Barton persisted in introducing his guests to each other, which, as the author comments, was in bad taste, since they were all Bostonians. One gentleman objected to this interference with social custom and bluntly told Barton that he must decline to accept the acquaintance of the person to whom he was presented. It was explained to Barton that there had been a deadly feud between the two men caused by a disagreement over a cargo of saltpetre. In spite of this, the men had to sit next to each other at table, where they discoursed gunpowder slantwise. Other couples were just as badly mismated. In the comments of Mrs. Hastings, a country cousin from Hastingsville, is found an accurate estimate of the general incongruity of the whole affair.

In her opinion, "the old dinners were vastly pleasanter and better; for her part she liked to know what she was eating; nobody could tell what these Frenchmen did when they once got into one's kitchen. 'And then, cousin Barton, a good creature enough, and his wife even better, were thrown away upon the upper ten thousand.' They despised them, and melancholy to relate, by courting these people they had lost all their old friends. Now if you could have seen Nick at his own board years ago; he was such a happy fellow! urging everybody to eat his good things, and enjoying himself hugely; now he looks all curled up into a heap. . . . 'This all comes,' said she, . . . 'of spoling children. My cousin's daughters are all the time tutoring their parents, and have deprived them of all their pleasures.' "†

Mrs. Otis's novel, though not as amusing and written with as light a touch as *The Fortune Hunter*, is a careful reproduction of social situations in the Boston of her time seen through feminine

---

*Otis, Mrs. Harrison G.—"The Barclays of Boston", Boston, 1854, 209.
†ibid., p. 261.

eyes.   It shows the presence there already of definite and sharply-outlined coteries, and it shows also the attempts of newer groups to invade the aristocratic circles, attempts which were noted in New York by Cooper and condemned by him.   To Mrs. Otis the situation seemed less serious, for, like Mrs. Mowatt, she accepted it as a matter of course, but nevertheless thought it a worthy topic for light satire.

Social life in the city during the Civil War was swept away from its customary routine of pleasurable entertainments.   The few contemporary accounts of it which are preserved in the novel witness to this fact.   Two novels by Henry Morford—*Shoulder Straps* (1863) and *The Days of Shoddy* (1863) aim to describe New York life of the war days, but they leave the reader with a rather confused impression of that life.   Social relationships receive little attention, and there is no attempt to depict the varied social classes in existence in the city at the time.   The plots are melodramatic in nature as are also the conversations of the characters in the more tense scenes.

S. Weir Mitchell, writing about twenty years after the close of the war, produced two novels, *In War Time* (1884) and *Roland Blake* (1886), which were greatly superior to Morford's efforts. The first, however, has few city scenes, since the Germantown where most of the action takes place, was at the time located outside Philadelphia city limits and was not as now a well-populated suburban section.   In *Roland Blake,* New York becomes the scene for some of the quieter incidents, but there is a very evident absence of those moments of gayety and splendor that are the usual accompaniment of social activities in the city of normal times.   One must, therefore, look to novels that describe life some years after the close of the war to find a resumption of detailed attention to social affairs.

In two novels by Mrs. H. B. Stowe one may find good illustrations of this revival of interest.   They offer repetition of a topic for satire already noted: the artificial distinctions that determine the various grades of social life.   In *My Wife and I,* the Van Arsdels are declared to belong to the upper tens, "not the oldest Tens, but the second batch.   Not the old Knickerbocker Vanderhoof, and Vanderhyde, and Vanderhorn set . . . but the modern nobs."* The head of the family is an importer "worth his millions." The education of the girls is obtained at a college where they teach girls everything that ever has been heard of, before they are seventeen, and then they are sent to France, Germany and Italy to pick up "all the languages; so that when they have anything to say they have a choice of four languages to say it in."† It is apparent that here the former insistence upon birth and family tradition as a requirement for entrance into the city social world has been somewhat lessened, and that the "modern nobs" have succeeded in attaining to full recognition. This is seen in the description of one of them, Eva Van Arsdel, as "a New York princess of the blood," and a "Fifth Avenue princess who has the world of fashion at her feet." The name Van Arsdel suggests that the family was of the proper Dutch extraction, but the assignment to Mr. Van Arsdel of millions gained in business shows that the family was not entirely resting upon traditions but desired to add wealth to its qualifications for leadership. Their home, however, is evidence of the genuineness of their claim, for it is not like the vulgarly ornamented residence of a Mrs. Jarvis *(Home as Found)* or of the Bartons *(The Barclays of Boston)*; on the contrary, it is a palatial house elegantly furnished and ornamented with works of art that show the real taste of the owners.

Eva's engagement to Harry Henderson, a rising young journalist, was a step downward in the social scale, since he was without either family distinction or wealth. Unlike many rich girls of the novels of that time, she preferred love to social prestige. When her father fails in business, there is, of course, no longer any question of sacrifice of social position. She and Harry are now on equal footing. During their early married life as described in *We and Our Neighbors,* they live on an unfashionable street and mingle freely with a heterogeneous gathering consisting of a Quaker woman-preacher, a Jewish rabbi, an Episcopalian minister, a happy-go-lucky journalist, and two old-fashioned elderly ladies. The last two were sisters and Vanderhaydens; they had been taught to revere the old approved English classics like Young's

---

*Stowe, Mrs. Harriet B.—"My Wife and I" (1871), Riverside edition, 168.
†ibid., 169.

Night Thoughts, but contrived now and then to obtain cheap editions of Dickens in order "to see what people were reading in these trashy times." All these formed a most diversified social group whom the Hendersons courageously attempted to pacify while entertaining them in their home. Mrs. Stowe had here a splendid theme for her skilful pen, but unfortunately she seemed unable to make effective use of it. Indeed, the same criticism may be made of the whole novel, that it is rather ineffective because its interests are too far-flung and there is no concentration.

Apparent differences of social rank likewise are important in the development of the story of Henry James's *Washington Square.* This novel is noteworthy for the fact that it bears an extremely inviting title but contains a very tiresome story. It carries the reader back about thirty years and then progresses forward to about 1870. In all this time the conservative Slopers, father and daughter, have not changed a great deal in character, but Catherine has had her happiness ruined by her father's obstinate refusal to permit her to marry young Morris Townsend, whom she loves. Dr. Sloper objects to him because he is without money or position and was reported to have squandered a small inheritance in a life of dissipation, and above all, the doctor objects to him because Morris, he believes, is no gentleman. As a matter of fact, he has few real qualifications to commend him aside from his engaging presence. Catherine never marries and before the age of forty has become an old-fashioned person, and an authority on customs that have passed away. She was greatly liked by the younger portion of the Washington Square set as a sort of kindly maiden-aunt. The girls found that they could safely confide their love affairs to her, and the young men became fond of her without knowing why. She became eccentric and extremely conservative on all moral and social matters. Her character seems to fit in admirably with the Sloper home as James describes it, "a handsome, modern, wide-fronted house, with a big balcony before the drawing-room windows, and a flight of white marble steps ascending to a portal which was also faced with white marble,"* The house was built in 1835. Its charac-

---

*James, Henry, Jr.—"Washington Square", New York, 1881, 23.

teristics—dignity, elegance, intellectuality, and coldness—describe exactly the Catherine Sloper of 1870 as she sits in the front parlor overlooking Washington Square and its established repose. Morris Townsend is now forty-five, but still has a fine appearance, a fair and lustrous beard and a handsome face. As he enters the old house where he courted Catherine many years before, the reader foresees the cold disdain with which the unemotional Catherine will greet him. She has become as obstinate as her father. There is no apparent reason why she should not now accept his friendly advances, for they are now both free, but she remembers that he once treated her badly, and tells him that she cannot forget the great change that made in her life. He goes away angry, never to return, and she in the parlor has again taken up her "morsel of fancy-work" and has "seated herself with it again—for life, as it were." This is one of James's poorest novels, as he himself understood, but it is memorable for at least one thing: its unflinching portrayal of an uninspiring, narrow-minded, convention-loving spinster who seems to fit admirably the particular section of the city into which James has placed her.

In the same year as *Washington Square,* Edgar Fawcett wrote a novel entitled *A Gentleman of Leisure,* which called attention to a contemporary weakness of American life especially noticeable in the cities, namely, an excessive reverence for English manners and customs. Two other novels in the decade, 1881-1890, gave considerable attention to the same phenomenon. These were Fawcett's *Olivia Delaplaine* (1888) and Mrs. Burton Harrison's *The Anglomaniacs* (1890). The list could be greatly augmented by selection from these and other writers specializing in contemporary American life, but the three novels named have been chosen as being thoroughly representative of the tendency as it affected the lives of people of the city. New York is the scene of all three.

In *A Gentleman of Leisure* the principal character, Clinton Wainwright, is gradually transformed from a scoffer of America and a dyed-in-the-wool sympathizer with England into an American patriot of the first water. It was in New York city that he received the transforming influences and it was there that he met and contested verbally with an obstinate addict of Anglomania who was declared to be only one of a large clique of men like him. Wainwright's love affair with Ruth Cheever was one of the greatest reasons for his realization of the superiority of his own country to that of England, where he had long resided. But once convinced of that fact, he was not slow in defending America against all its detractors. One in particular, at the Metropolitan Club, aroused his anger. This was Gansevoort, who, the author writes, "walked, talked, sat down, got up, smoked his cigar, and carried his umbrella precisely like an Englishman, and yet the trained vision of Wainwright saw that it was all spurious mannerism, and not unconscious habit." Wainwright and Gansevoort came almost to blows at their club; the former was entirely willing to accommodate his opponent if he wished to have satisfaction, but whether the accommodation called for fists, swords, or pistols was not disclosed, since the dispute was suddenly dropped.

In *Olivia Delaplaine*, Fawcett's satire of American worship of English life takes the form of showing young men of fashion in New York aping English fashions in clothes and manners, and in recreations. The Gotham younger social set apologize for their coaches parade which is forced to start in Madison Square because they have no better substitute for Hyde Park, London. To Jasper Masserene, born of American mother and English father and educated at Cambridge University, the New York parade does seem a small affair and he disapproves heartily of this aping of a custom so essentially English. Soon he too, like Wainwright, becomes Americanized and chooses for wife an American woman, one who was also educated abroad but has a deep respect for American institutions and American people. A counterpart to Gansevoort in unrelenting adherence to English fashion is found in this novel in young Aspinwall Satterthwaite, who though a member of an old Knickerbocker family, "wanted above all imaginable things to be English." His snobbish manners and dissipated habits make him unworthy to bear the name of either Englishman or American.

Fawcett's method of opposing Anglomania was to show its gradual disappearance from an individual's life in the face of his increased veneration for American people and their customs. In *A Gentleman of Leisure* he devotes much more attention to Anglo-

mania than he does in *Olivia Delaplaine,* but the impression left
with the reader after finishing both books is that the author believes that the craze is not, after all, a very dangerous menace to
the city's social life. In the former novel he glides easily and
gracefully away from the subject after a few telling smashes at
it in the person of Gansevoort, and enters upon a more brilliant
and more forceful denunciation of other shortcomings of Fifth
Avenue life. Anglomania becomes in *Olivia Delaplaine* a subordinate element and is assigned to minor characters. Knowing
Fawcett's admiration for Henry James, who was a great wor-
shipper at the shrine of things English, one does not marvel at
his reluctance to stand out boldly against Anglomania. Fawcett
himself at the age of fifty followed the example of James and
went to England, where he lived until his death in 1904. His
thrusts against American fondness for English manners and customs, although placed in entertaining fiction, were not as effective
as the keener attacks of Mrs. Harrison.

The Anglomaniacs was a more severe arraignment of the folly
than either of the novels of Fawcett just considered. There is in
it a great deal of exaggeration of the habits of rich New Yorkers
and of their vulgar display of wealth. Mrs. Harrison achieved
thereby a more striking work than *A Gentleman of Leisure* and
a more powerful protest. It is purely a novel of purpose and,
somewhat unusual in a city novel, it concentrates upon one phase
of city conduct. One does not feel that Mrs. Harrison was
writing as faithful a picture of city life as Fawcett or that she was
his equal in craftmanship; but one is certain that her satire was,
on the whole, more efficacious. In *The Anglomaniacs* she shows
the folly for things English too deeply ingrained in the minds and
habits of her characters to allow them to relinquish it. Looking
at the novel from the viewpoint of present-day conditions when
Anglomania no longer threatens the social life of the city, one
cannot help being amused at the curious habits and thoughts
which, according to Mrs. Harrison, it aroused in the 1880's. At
the beginning of the story, Mrs. Floyd-Curtis, returning from
England, expresses her disdain for her native New York in sen-
tences like the following:

"Actually, the whole thing seems more dingy and deplorable to me every time I come back. Such a dreadful rattle in one's ears, the side-walks so filthy and obstructed, the lower classes so presuming, and the sun glaring so that you can't help seeing everything."*

New York's fondness for titled persons is described by a good-natured clubman as follows: . . . . "the title hunt goes on with undiminished zeal. Every little sprig of nobility they send over to us from the other side is made much of in New York, and then passed along through the other cities."† Mrs. Floyd-Curtis insists that her daughter become engaged to one of them, a Lord Melrose, even though it necessitates the dissolution of an incipient romance with a middle-class Englishman who has come to this country to take a professorship in a small college. The girl was in love with this "commoner" but had no affection whatever for the "sprig of nobility." Her mother, however, uses the acquaintanceship with the Melrose family to strengthen her social position in the city. Already she had gained a real footing in the social world by her elaborate, luxurious entertainments, but "the fortnight's visit from the Countess of Melrose before going to the West convinced New Yorkers of Mrs. Floyd-Curtis's real merit. If there had been any lingering hesitancy on this question, the arrival of the young Earl, and the business-like way in which he proceeded to attach himself to the Floyd-Curtis train would have removed it."‡

Mrs. Floyd-Curtis is another example of the *nouveau riche* element in the city, for she and her husband, who was in the dry-goods business, had lived in quiet circumstances in New York for twelve years. A sudden acquisition of fortune on her part by inheritance changed her whole life and led her into a mania for foreign fashions. It is not true of all who are affected by Anglomania that they are of the newly rich class, but as may be noted in Fawcett's novels, the worship of things English was indulged in also by young Knickerbockers like Aspinwall Satterthwaite.

William D. Howells excels his fellow-novelists in dealing with the social scene as he did with the struggle for success. Varia-

---

*Harrison, Mrs. Burton, "The Anglomaniacs", New York, 1890, 2-3.
†ibid., 76.
‡ibid., 182.

tions in social classes are frequently noted in his novels just as they were in the novels of the other writers already studied. For a good illustration of this, one may turn to *A Modern Instance*. The distinction there is made by Clara Kingsbury, who represents one of Boston's well-established families. She plans to entertain for the first time Bartley Hubbard and his wife, but does not desire to be thought to recognize them as of equal rank with her most intimate friends who belong to old Boston families. Her procedure on this, as on other occasions of a similar nature, was to invite as her guests to meet the newcomers to her drawing-room only those of her friends who were not particularly fashionable. The Hubbards had a very unpleasant time, for with the acumen of most people in such situations, they recognized at once the quality of the guests assembled to greet them and were greatly chagrined to realize that their hostess thought them unworthy to associate with her friends from the élite. To be forced to spend the evening with the second best among her acquaintances did not at all please them or comport with their dignity. To cap the climax, Miss Kingsbury served only tea and cakes; consequently, they both came home hungry, since they had expected a regular full-course dinner.*

Contrast in social rank is again made the theme of Howells' art in the entertainment by Bromfield Corey and his wife in honor of the Laphams, whose claim to recognition by their fellow-men is bound up with Silas's success in business, or, in other words, with money. The Coreys are much better fortified socially They come from Boston's oldest families. The invitation to the Laphams comes as a result of the intimacy of Tom Corey with the Lapham daughters. The evening would probably have passed without any unpleasant incident if Silas had not partaken too freely of wine—a drink to which he is unaccustomed, since only ice-water is served at his home. The scene in the Corey library

---

*In Robert Grant's *Unleavened Bread* (1900) Selma Littleton and her husband are treated in a similar way by the Williamses who were formerly their neighbors in the city until they moved into a smarter neighborhood. At the dinner in the new home to which they are invited, the Littletons find that the guests are only people whom they know already; Selma is bitter against her former associates, because she understands that she and her husband are not thought good enough to meet their new friends.

after dinner when Lapham gradually loses his control over his senses is one memorable for its quiet pathos. He has lost his awe at the strangeness of dining in real society and has acquired an unwonted dignity. Soon he is calling Corey by his first name and is discoursing fluently on his taste for books and painting, about which, as a matter of fact, his knowledge is extremely slight. He dominates the scene so that no one else dares to interrupt him. Unconsciously he is making himself more and more obnoxious as he changes to a topic in which he is entirely familiar: the manner in which he has made a million dollars in Boston from his paint business. One notes the gradual bursting of gates that normally bar man's inner thoughts from outward expression. Confident now that he has somehow been delegated to amuse and entertain all the others, Lapham blurts out the first words that come to his mind and is only saved from disgracing himself before his hostess to whom he tries to bid good-night by the quick action of Tom Corey, who leads him out of the house by a side-door. One's sympathies are aroused the more easily for Lapham because one realizes that he is a man naturally kind-hearted and deeply considerate of the rights of others, and that solely as a result of his inexperience with dinners in fashionable homes he has fallen a victim to the wine served there. His is distinctly an error of the amateur or beginner; and it is all the more pathetic in that it comes to a man of his mature years and common sense.

Howells fully understood how a gentleman will instinctively act when confronted with another's humiliating confession of personal misbehavior. This is seen in his realistic handling of the scene that takes place between Silas Lapham and young Tom Corey the day after the dinner at which the older man disgraced himself so unfortunately. Tom feels a strong disgust with Lapham, not only for his uncouth conduct the night before, but also for his frankness in discussing that conduct with him. He has been trained to pay no undue attention to an offense committed by a guest in his father's home. Therefore, he intimates delicately that every man at the dinner understood perfectly that Lapham had not been quite himself because he was not accustomed to the drinking of wine. Further than that, Tom will not discuss the

question, though all the time he is becoming more and more disturbed by the Colonel's words. He represses his real feelings
and makes a hurried departure. His conduct on this occasion is
what one would expect of him, but few novelists handling a similar situation would have been as careful as Howells to have their
characters act in such a repressed manner. In dealing with scenes
of that nature, the temptation is to make them as violent as possible, but in so doing the authors disregard the fact that in actual
life a man's humiliation before another man is a distressing experience for the latter, and that he desires to escape from it as quickly
as Tom Corey did. Howells' method is more impressive for its
use of brevity and simplicity, and for its faithful adherence to the
real facts of life. Not many novelists have followed his example,
fearing perhaps that by use of like restraint they will be guilty
of dullness. It is, in fact, a difficult method and one which only
a skilled craftsman can properly handle.

In *The Minister's Charge* a contrast is made between twenty-
year-old, rural-bred Lemuel Barker and city-bred patricians like
the Coreys and the Bellinghams. Mr. Corey desires to obtain a
young man to read to him because his eye sight is failing. A
cousin, the bachelor Charles Bellingham, undertakes the task of
offering the position to Barker. His method of doing this by
inviting the young man to breakfast with him in his expensive
bachelor apartment provides the author with the opportunity of
drawing interesting comparisons between the awed young rustic
and the three others present about the table. The host had invited
also two of his best friends—Meredith, a lawyer, and Seyton, an
Anglican minister. All of them treat Lemuel as an equal, so that
his unfamiliarity with a fashionable bachelor's breakfast at nine
o'clock in the morning is presumably unnoticed. He had never
imagined a morning meal like that—it was indeed bountiful with
its shad, broiled chicken, lamb chops, omelet, bread and butter
and, at the close, a dish of strawberries. The talk was lively and
bantering. Lemuel took little part in it until he was compelled
to answer delicate queries of the others about the recent fire at
which newspaper accounts had described him as playing the part
of hero. Howells is here picturing the courteous actions of real
gentlemen skilled in the polite art of making themselves agreeable

to one who is of an inferior class socially. They are so sincere that Barker is not at all embarrassed when Bellingham asks him to read a short selection from Bret Harte's story *How Christmas Came to Simpson's Bar*. The request comes quite naturally in the course of conversation, and it is not till later that Bellingham, impressed by Barker's intelligent reading, offers him the situation in the Corey home. There he found himself dropped into the midst of a luxury stranger to him than the strange things he found in the novels he had to read to his employer. Strange too, in his opinion, was the conduct of the Corey family with reference to him. Although they were always polite and kind to him when he met them in the library, they seemed to show no curiosity about him. At first he wondered that Mr. Corey's two daughters had not been chosen to read to their father but, as Howells slyly interpolates, he did not know "the disability for mutual help that riches bring." Barker himself soon observed this phenomenon when he saw how much the daughters were engrossed with charity and art, or social cares, and then he understood that "they could not have rendered nor their father have received from his family the duty which he was paid to do, as they must have done if they had been poorer."*

Barker's experiences in the elegant home of the Coreys are thus used by Howells to introduce lightly satirical references to certain discrepancies in the home life of one of Boston's most aristocratic families. These are universal characteristics of such city homes, namely: the unfailing politeness of the inmates to their social inferiors mingled at the same time with a certain haughty indifference; the inability of individual members of the family to help one another in solving problems as they arise in the home—an inability which is explained by the fact that each is engrossed in his own participation in the life of the city outside the home. Hence, when an unforeseen change in the family routine is seen approaching, outside assistance has to be summoned.

In *April Hopes* (1888) Howells is writing almost entirely about the life of people of wealth and social distinction. The two principal families are the Pasmers and the Maverings. The

---

*Howells, William D.—"The Minister's Charge", Boston, 1887, 382.

former are declared by Dan Mavering, who is in love with Alice Pasmer, to be connected with the best families in Boston and to be in the best society, but owing to long residence in Europe they have acquired a certain independence which the ordinary Bostonians do not have. Thus they think it not beneath their dignity to live in a flat instead of a large house on Commonwealth Avenue or Beacon Street. The Maverings too are rich people but live in the country. When Mrs. Pasmer, with her daughter, visits them, she notes the rustic conceit of Dan's parents and sisters and exclaims at the house as being "perfectly baronial —and ridiculous." To her city-trained mind, it seems utterly wasted in the country, where no great entertainments can be held bringing in "troops of guests." There all it connotes is money.

Probably the most noteworthy social event described in *April Hopes* is the reception at Mrs. James Bellingham's, a function marked by a lack of genuine warmth of hospitality. Bromfield Corey, who is a regular visitor to Howells' city novels, is here shown in a philosophical mood commenting on the people who come to the reception and upon his hostess, who is also his sister-in-law. Corey seems to have aged considerably even since his last appearance in connection with Sewell and Lemuel Barker. Now he is declared to be sixty-nine years of age. Perhaps his advancing years have made him cynical. At any rate, his judgment of the Bellingham reception is unsparing in its disapproval of the lack of attention paid by the hostess to her guests. He declares to Mrs. Brinkley in a tone of voice that others nearby could not choose but hear: "Jane's idea of society is to turn a herd of human beings loose in her house, and see what will come of it. She has no more sense of hospitality or responsibility than the Elements or Divine Providence. You may come here and have a good time—if you can get it; she won't object; or you may die of solitude and inanition; she'd never know it . . . she'd be grieved if she thought any one went away unhappy, but she does nothing to make them at home in her house—absolutely nothing."*

*Howells, William D.—"April Hopes," New York, 1888, 309-10.

With reference to the treatment of strangers at these receptions, Corey is just as vehement in denunciation. . . . "If you ask a stranger to your house, you establish a tacit understanding with him that you won't forget him after you have him there . . . the theory is that, being turned loose here and with the rest, they may speak to anybody; but the fact is, they can't. . . . There ought to be policemen, to show strangers about and be kind to them. . . . "*

One may well believe that in these words of Corey, Howells is uttering in an indirect manner his own criticism of the exclusiveness and general clannishness of Boston social functions of the time.   Events that occur at the reception verify the judgment of Corey, for Mavering finds former acquaintances of his being ignored. He rescues them and devotes considerable time to their entertainment, for which on the next day he reaps his reward in the form of the return of his engagement ring by Alice Pasmer.

Another rich family with social aspirations, but infinitely less refined than the Laphams, is the Dryfoos family in *A Hazard of New Fortunes*. Books of etiquette are not capable of guiding this western Pennsylania family into New York social life, so a personal interpreter is obtained for them in Mrs. Mandell, a native of Brooklyn. Her task—a difficult one as it proves—is to care for them not only socially but economically, as their housekeeper, and to help them acquire as much as possible of urban polish. She cannot accomplish a great deal with them. The daughters, whom the father was so anxious to introduce into New York's oldest and most exclusive homes, were totally unable to meet the standards necessary for such a promotion. Their main deficiencies—in education and manners—proved to be insuperable barriers preventing their acceptance. Their fundamental misconception of city social values is seen in their belief that New York is unsociable because no one comes to call upon them; and when Miss Vance, out of pity for their loneliness does make a call, they at once get the impression that her visit is inspired by a desire to be the first to get on good terms with

*ibid., 310.

them since the city has learned of their father's great wealth. And when invited to a *musicale* at Mrs. Horn's, they conduct themselves so rudely that their hostess, a power in New York society, determines not to have the reputation of her gatherings again endangered by their presence. The girls are thereafter left to work out their own social progress. Howells does not carry his story far enough to show their ultimate success or failure in New York social circles, for, as already noted, the family went abroad and scored brilliantly in foreign circles where they had failed so signally at home. The reader is left with the implication that they were not greatly different from others, who once just as uncultivated, did eventually secure a permanent place in good society. This impression is clearly made by Basil March when he declares to his wife after this same function:

"Such people as the Dryfooses are the raw material of good society. It isn't made up of refined or meritorious people—professors and litterateurs, ministers and musicians, and their families. All the fashionable people there tonight were like the Dryfooses a generation or two ago. I dare say the material works up faster now, and in a season or two you won't know the Dryfooses from the other plutocrats."

A cynical point of view, of course, but one which was far from being an exaggeration, if one is to accept the picture of urban society presented by most of the writers of fiction.

Howells displayed keen knowledge of social problems of city life and admirable ability in picturing and analyzing them. His outstanding success in this respect in my opinion, and of course this is only a personal preference, is his account of the visit of the Laphams to the home of the Coreys for dinner, when Silas commits the social blunder of over-indulgence in wine. In this scene, as in his other efforts at depicting social life, he displayed conservatism, and sincerity. He was never betrayed by personal prejudice into severe, unjust condemnation of the faults of any single class in the city social world as were Cooper and Lippard, and later, his contemporaries, Fawcett and Mrs. Harrison, nor did he fall into the mistake of overpraise. In style, he is superior to most of his contemporaries with the exception of Henry James. He never indulges in trite, commonplace language; in this he is unlike many of the writers of city novels who seem to think that an absorbing plot will compensate for lack of distinction in diction. The best test of Howells' thorough superiority is the fact that one can return with profit time and again to his pictures of social life and discover interesting side-lights that one missed on the previous reading. With most of his contemporaries writing on the same theme, this is not true. With Fawcett, especially, one feels no inclination to revive scenes by a second reading of them.

The year 1886 brought the publication of *The Story of Margaret Kent* by Mrs. Ellen Olney Kirk under the pen name of Henry Hayes. This was a novel with a distinctly social flavor and one which deserved its unusual popularity because of its straightforward presentation of the struggle within the soul of a married woman to decide between her duty to remain by her husband, worthless though he was, and her desire to satisfy her keen social and intellectual ambitions, which she knew could be admirably accomplished by divorce and re-marriage to a man who was more congenial to her. The problem of divorce, even in the wicked city, was not usually discussed so openly and fully in the novel of the eighties as it is in the present-day novel. Consequently, Mrs. Kirk's book created somewhat of a sensation for indulgence in a dangerous subject. Today that subject is all too common in fiction, but the book still has its value in picturing in an entertaining manner the difficult path which a newcomer must pursue before he or she can hope to obtain full social recognition in the inner circles of a large city.

Margaret Kent came to New York city from the South; she soon found herself thrown upon her own resources when her husband Robert Kent went to South America to make his fortune after having first squandered most of the money that his wife had inherited from her father. Margaret is not nearly so helpless as Helen Harkness was in *A Woman's Reason*. She had literary talent and was in addition possessed of a very attractive personality. She did not obtain a permanent place in the city's literary world, and the references in the novel to this part of her career are not nearly so convincing as the scenes describing her social struggles. The great desire of her life was for social conquest. In this she was greatly handicapped because of the fact that the city's exclusive circles took little notice of her. Her husband's apparent desertion of her threw a blot upon her reputation, and this was darkened by the persistent rumors that she had accepted financial aid from several young men of wealth and position. The rumors were hardly just to Margaret, though it was true that her afternoons at home were always well attended by young men, several of whom were in love with her. But her real fondness was for association with other women, which, to her regret, was generally denied her. One woman who invited her often to social functions was Mrs. Townsend of whose safe place in society Mrs. Kent was somewhat jealous. Mrs. Townsend was the typical gossip-bearer always found in city life, and was thus a most dangerous companion. Margaret's social success was gained in the face of this woman's innuendos and came about principally through her charm of manner and her animated, intelligent conversation. Complete triumph was delayed by the return of the long-absent husband, whose disgraceful conduct made him entirely unacceptable to polite society. Ultimately she achieved her goal but not until after Kent's death in the South of yellow fever. That she ever attained social recognition in the city was owing not to wealth or breeding but to the clever manipulation of whatever talents and resources she found ready for her use.

A novel with such a definite emphasis upon the social life of the city was not, of course, without its references to the intrusion of newer and unwelcome elements into the placidity of the old and traditional circles. This is found in the complaint of Mrs. Devereux that she now has trouble in finding any one she knows in New York society. She declares . . . "although people are unfamiliar, they need not be so hideously unfamiliar as those McElraths . . . They were dreadful . . . they all had tusks . . . I felt myself in a den of wild beasts . . . And they were all so pleased to see me, and so enormously polite—I say enormously, for nothing else seems to express it, they all opened their great cavernous mouths so wide and showed their tusks so frightfully."*

---

*Kirk, Mrs. Ellen Olney—"The Story of Margaret Kent", New York, 1886, 220-221.

Satire of the older elements of New York society is seen also in the character of Mrs. Sinclair, the cousin of Margaret Kent, who resented her presence in the city, penniless and without a husband to protect her. She cannot understand why there should be people without money or why a man should be on one side of the equator and his wife on the other. Margaret is invited to the Sinclair home only to family dinners, at which the food is rather scarce, somewhat as it was when Clara Kingsbury entertained the Hubbards in *A Modern Instance.* When Mrs. Sinclair learns of facts derogatory to Robert Kent's character and advises Margaret to take steps to divorce him, she suggests that Margaret leave New York and journey to some quiet spot out West and there have the divorce arranged. In all this she is actuated by a fear that the Kents, husband or wife, will mar the hitherto unspotted honor of her family by the notoriety which divorce proceedings will arouse in the city newspapers.

The Story of Margaret Kent throws light upon the life of women primarily, but in Mrs. Kirk's *Queen Money* (1888) the emphasis is upon man's activities both in business and in society. Otto March, unlike Margaret Kent, does not have to scheme and contrive in order to obtain social recognition in New York: he has it thrust upon him, for he "was born with a gold spoon in his mouth," and moreover is a Knickerbocker—a Vandewaters. The highest circles of society are opened to him without question. At a dinner of millionaires given by the eccentric Colonel Carver, he receives a magnificent gold watch from the host who was evidently endeavoring to create a record for the amount of money that could be spent upon one entertainment. Otto's was the costliest souvenir, though all the guests, thirty in number, received elaborate novelties. The other millionaires also take a strong fancy to the young man, and one by one they offer him a yacht for an entire season all expenses paid; or a summer home on the same conditions; or a shooting-box in New Jersey as an outright gift; or two valuable dogs, or a fine-blooded mare. Through all this Otto remains unspoiled. Mrs. Kirk is here, of course, exaggerating the habits of rich city people, but her idealistic picture is not uninviting; indeed, it is quite attractive, just as the pictures of wealthy city life presented by Crawford and Warner are attractive.

Otto March is not so much of a creation as Margaret Kent, but like her he is not goody-goody. He has his moments of weakness. His faults are rather youthful and peculiarly urban. In his earlier days in the city while in attendance at the theatre he had become fascinated with Maud Campion, a celebrated actress and dancer of uncertain age. When he sees her name on the hand-bag of a young woman riding on the Elevated, he follows her home, then sends her six bouquets of flowers in rapid succession and continues to go every night to the theatre. He thinks that the actress is wearing his flowers but is gravely disillusioned when he finally gets courage enough to call at Maud Campion's house, for he discovers that the young girl is in fact Maud Campion but not the actress. In spite of this unfortunate commencement, an intimacy springs up between the two, thus providing the author with a good opportunity for social contrast, of which she makes effective use. The girl, uneducated and almost destitute of male companionship, finds Otto a veritable "fairy prince on a white steed." Her tastes, however, are entirely different from his; they are little better suited to one another than were Statira Dudley and Lemuel Barker. Otto is more fortunate than Lemuel, for he makes a fortunate and even honorable escape from her. The heroine Lucy Florian, a girl more suitable for him socially and intellectually, exerts a strong influence upon him through her sage warning against "that wicked thirst for money" prevalent among the business men with whom he has to mingle.

Both of these novels by Mrs. Kent are marked by the reality and sincerity of their social scenes. Their tone is not too pessimistic as to the quality of social standards then prevailing in a city such as New York, nor is it too optimistic. The reader obtains a clear idea of what the actual conditions in the city were at the time, though the picture is somewhat idealized now and then. The narratives are engrossing and not at all sensational to the present-day sophisticated reading public. The author's style is entirely adequate though not distinctive.

In the twenty or more novels of New York city life written by Edgar Fawcett the theme of social contrast predominates. One finds him satirizing both the snobbish behavior of the Knicker-bocker aristocracy and also the boldness of the newly rich. He was usually able to write stories that gripped his readers' attention, but unfortunately he did not seem able to produce works that had enduring qualities. His characters are generally typical of real persons one often meets in the city. The average reader recognizes them, but owing to the fact that they do not have any marks of real distinction, he does not feel more than a passing interest in them. Perhaps Fawcett wrote too much. At any rate, the fact remains that his social novels have altogether lost their former popularity. *A Gentleman of Leisure, Olivia Delaplaine* and *A Man's Will* have already been noticed, the first two for their connection with Anglomania and the last for its picture of the problem of intemperance. In *The House at High Bridge* (1887) Fawcett was writing about a family which was in itself a strange contradiction in social values, for the husband, Herbert Coggeshall, a novelist, belonged remotely to such people as the Van Twillers, the Van Corlears and the Ten Eycks, but his wife was the daughter of a man "who kept a popular eating-house not far from Bowling Green." They live in modest circumstances in High Bridge, a New York suburb, not through preference but necessity. Their lives while quite commonplace as compared with the rich Satterthwaites and Auchinclosses of *Olivia Delaplaine,* are just as typical of their particular class in the social scale as are the former. One daughter, Isabel, intellectual like her father, after education in Europe, returns to New York completely "at home in good society and well versed in all its arbitrary regulations." The other daughter, Sadie, is entirely different, taking her characteristics from her mother who is more or less "ordinary" and materialistic. The best social scene is one in which the commonplace members of the family take part in a luncheon given by Mrs. Coggeshall in honor of Sadie's prospective mother-in-law, Mrs. Coulter, a woman who is still lower in the social world than her hostess. It is from Mrs. Coulter that the humor of the affair emanates, namely, from her constant boasting about her children and her illusions about her former days on East Broadway at her "old family-mansion", which, as the reader quickly learns, was no more than a large boarding-house. This attention to a lower order of gentility in city life is not common with Fawcett, though touches of it may also be found in *Olivia Delaplaine,* in the episodes taking place in Mrs. Ottarson's boarding-house. On the whole, one prefers his pictures of the so-called upper classes. There he seems more at home. In *The House at High Bridge* the characters are typical suburban dwellers with the normal social problems of suburban life and the usual dissatisfaction on the part of some because they must live on the outskirts of the metropolitan centre which is for them the only source of pleasure and happiness. But something more than the typical, the usual, and the normal is needed for a novelist like Fawcett to make a really attractive novel of this kind of life.

Frank R. Stockton, whose interest was usually in an imaginary world of fantasy, wrote on several occasions upon the contemporary city scene. In *The Hundredth Man* (1887), for example, he satirizes, somewhat in the manner of Fawcett, the snobbishness of the city rich as personified by Mr. Stull, a bank president. Stull is the owner of a highly profitable New York restaurant, which though not by any means a rival of Delmonico's, caters to a rather select patronage. This fact does not prevent its proprietor from feeling it a disgrace that he should have made most of his wealth through the restaurant business. In order that no one shall learn of his connection with Vatoldi's, thus endangering his well-established post in the New York social world, he keeps that fact a secret. But his scheme to remain known as a banker and yet reap the huge profits of a restaurant keeper is shattered in the course of the novel. In the end he has to accede to his ultra-modern daughter's demand that he give up Vatoldi's, so that she and her fiance will not be socially ruined. The latter's employment by a mercantile house makes him highly objectionable to Stull as a son-in-law, but inasmuch as his daughter has learned his secret, he has no other course to follow than to yield. He now has to find new outlets for his money, and in the manner of rich men of the city like C. D. Warner's "Uncle Jerry" Hollowell* and Henderson* he plans to place it in a great

---

*"Uncle Jerry" Hollowell, railway magnate in *A Little Journey in the World* aimed to divert the public mind from the failure of some of his

enterprise that will attract universal attention to himself. For this purpose he plans a legal aid institution of which he expects to be the director-in-chief. Additional advertisement of himself will come from a marble slab in the entrance-hall bearing his name as founder.

Stockton's manner of treating social situations in the city is noteworthy for its combination of humor and satire. One can also see hints of his rich imagination in the midst of comparatively unattractive situations. It would have been a fortunate thing for the urban novel if a writer like Fawcett who was such an ardent admirer of the city, could have borrowed freely from Stockton's vast treasure-house of humor and fancy.

S. Weir Mitchell, whose Civil War novels have already been mentioned, wrote in 1892 *Characteristics,* a novel which reproduces in entertaining fashion the informal gatherings of men prominent in the social life of Philadelphia in the early nineties. The reader is attracted by the brilliance and the instructive qualities of their conversations. Dr. North is probably the most entertaining of the coterie on account of the strange medical histories that he vividly relates of cases personally observed by him in his practice. The others—St. Clair, a sculptor and poet, Vincent, a lawyer, and Clayborne, an historian and scholar—also contribute to the general entertainment by incidents derived from their own experience. The value of the book lies in the peculiar skill with which the author retains his reader's attention despite the thinness of the plot, and in the fact that it is a charming and informative account of the lives of men of the city who are able to obtain a satisfying recreation for themselves through the free exchange of facts and opinions acquired in the ordinary course of their professions. The reader feels that he is being introduced to persons of importance whom he has long wished to meet and whom he has admired for accomplishing great things for the community in an unostentatious manner. And after learning of the intellectual nature of the conversations which they share with

---

financial schemes by giving a bell to the Norembega Theological Institute. Henderson's philanthropies have already been noted. Both these men took special care to have their charitable activities prominently reported in the public press.

one another when secluded within their homes, he feels himself strengthened in his approval of them as human personalities.

In the New York novels of F. Marion Crawford—*Katharine Lauderdale* and *The Ralstons*—the reader may find well-drawn pictures of life in that city's social realm. With his customary interest in the unusual and romantic, Crawford reveals astonishing facts in regard to the lives of fabulously wealthy people of the city. His talent for creating a good story led him to select incidents that hold one's attention, and in addition, he appeared to be more keenly sympathetic with the persons of gentility about whom he was writing, than were Fawcett and Mrs. Harrison. He does not often indulge in social contrasts in these novels and in this respect is quite at variance with the general practice of his contemporaries. In thus confining his attentions to one social class—the highest—he seems to give a more accurate representation of that class, so that one feels that his work is to be relied upon for accuracy.

All the principal persons in these two novels by Crawford are connected either closely or remotely with the elderly Robert Lauderdale who is worth at least twenty-five millions. It will be helpful to name several instances of the unusual, almost unbelievable situations existing within this clan. According to common belief in New York city, it was a family that could command anything that it wanted at any time. The author reveals the true facts, showing that its fortune was not at all evenly distributed and its members not universally happy. Turning to the miserly Alexander Lauderdale, Jr., nephew of the millionaire, one learns that he claims to have no money outside of his small salary as manager of a trust fund. His routine takes him to business in downtown New York, but he spends only ten cents the whole day, that being necessary to pay his fare on the Elevated. He eats only two meals a day, one in the morning and the other at night. He borrows continually from his wife who herself earns a small income by painting miniatures—sufficient to buy clothes for herself and daughter Katharine. The latter and her uncle Robert believe that Alexander Jr. has secretly saved a large sum of money, possibly a million dollars, but that a passion for money-getting prevents him from spending it on his family as he should.

His tyrannical treatment of Katharine leads to her open revolt from him. His father, Alexander, Sr., is kept under strict surveillance and allowed almost no money because of his desire to appropriate every cent he can get towards the education of idiots. There are, of course, brighter moments in the lives of the younger people of the clan—Katharine Lauderdale and John Ralston. New York's entertainments, dinners, and balls are indicated not by long descriptions but by means of the intellectual conversations that take place there. Not all of these hold the reader's interest, but they are successful in creating a keener impression of what goes on at large city functions than the usual novelistic accounts with their undue emphasis upon the splendors of dress and decoration. Crawford no doubt felt that it would be sufficient if his characters talked and acted like flesh-and-blood men and women of urbanity and culture; it would not be necessary to label them as such and to paint in detail the richness and brilliancy of their surroundings.

The same absence of social contrast is found in the New York novels of Charles Dudley Warner. These have already been noted so fully that it is unnecessary to dwell upon them further. Like Crawford, Warner was concerned almost entirely with the activities of those whose position in the city had been obtained by acquisition of wealth. With his families the acquisition was more recent than it was with Crawford's, but nevertheless there was no snubbing of them by members of an older aristocratic clique. They are newly rich but are not troubled at all by lack of social adaptability as were the Dryfooses and the Laphams. Even the Hendersons, both of whom were newcomers to the city, were singularly triumphant socially. Perhaps they had passed the trying apprenticeship days to which Howells' *nouveau riche* succumbed. And one must remember that they were more wealthy than Howells' families, and could command the admiration of the city by their magnificent Fifth Avenue residences. With all their wealth, however, like Crawford's rich people, their private lives were far from happy, as already noted in a previous chapter.

The emphasis upon the social climber and the newly rich, and the contrast between their lives and the lives of old-established city families did not cease in the later years of the century. Edgar Fawcett and Mrs. Burton Harrison, among others, continued to dwell upon it, but the best illustration is undoubtedly to be found in Robert Grant's *Unleavened Bread* (1900). This novel contains remarkably realistic sketches of ambition on the part of several newcomers to New York, namely, Selma Littleton, wife of a rising young architect, and Flossy Williams and her husband, an enterprising stock-broker.

Although the story is laid back in the seventies, the problems treated are fundamentally the same as existed in the years contemporaneous with the date of publication. Selma Littleton comes to New York from the small city of Benham somewhere in the west about the same time as Flossy arrives from a city in New Jersey. They become neighbors in new, cheap houses in a side street west of the Park. Both husbands are New York men. Littleton understands the difficulties of promotion in the city and hence does not expect to reach the highest social circles unless it be by gaining an outstanding position in the city as an architect. Until that shall be attained, he is content to occupy a lower station, but Selma cannot understand why any New York families, even those living in the most exclusive of Fifth Avenue homes, should presume to consider themselves above her husband and herself. To her the whole urban system is un-American. But to Flossy Williams it is a thoroughly plausible system. She and her husband understand that at present they are only make-believe "swells", but they have a definite goal at which to aim: recognition by the Morton-Prices who belong to the ultra-conservative aristocratic set. They ultimately attain their goal by dint of Flossy's clever scheming and her husband's fortunate manipulation of the stock market. In the meantime, Selma's husband has concentrated on architecture and in a steady, plodding manner has risen to a high place in his profession. Selma has impeded him with her attempts to imitate Flossy's methods, not understanding that she, as a potential writer and he as a successful architect, were certain eventually of a secure place without lowering themselves to the use of such methods. The result is tragic for Littleton, as he succumbs to pneumonia, but Selma continues

her social struggles in another environment and attains a doubtful triumph as wife of a politician.

Perhaps the chief value of this novel to the present study is
the keen analysis it presents of the different grades of social
attainment in New York city.   Flossy Williams seems to be
the author's mouth-piece when she explains:

> "There's the conservative aristocratic set, the smart rapid set, the set
> which hasn't much money, but has Knickerbocker or other highly respectable
> ancestors, the new millionaire set, the literary set, the intellectual philan-
> thropic set, and so on, according to one's means or tastes. Each has its
> little circle which shades away into the others, and every now and then
> there is a big entertainment to which they all go."*

The able defence of these sets is worth noting also:

> "Most of the people in these different sets are somebodies because either
> their grandfathers or they have done something well—better than other
> people, and have made money as a consequence. And when a family has
> made money or won distinction by its brains . . . the members of it, even
> though dull, are entitled to respect . . . "†

Such a tolerant attitude is to be commended and is in marked
contrast with the attitude of many writers already reviewed whose
works seem to indicate that money is never an acceptable pass-
word for social admittance.   It is clear from this novel that
Judge Grant does not hesitate to uphold society's various distinctions; his criticism is not directed against them but against those
climbers who desire membership in sets to which they are not
qualified.   His work is commendable not only for clear analysis
of social values in the city, but also for its able characterizations
of two ambitious women, quite different in nature.

After reviewing the whole urban social scene as it has been
presented in this chapter, one may be somewhat doubtful of any
conclusions to be drawn therefrom.   The constant recurrence of
contrasts is the outstanding phenomenon.   By this frequent use
of comparisons, the novelists have striven to make their narratives
entertaining and vivid; and without them, in many cases, their

---

*Grant, Robert—"Unleavened Bread", New York, 1900, 146.
†ibid., 147.

works would have been able to secure only a minimum of attention.

What conclusions were reached with regard to the traditional city families? In answer, one must admit at once that there was no unanimity of opinion. Cooper was convinced of the right of such families to leadership, but in the one whom he upholds as city leader—Mrs. Hawker—one notes emphasis placed not only upon family tradition but also upon superiority in education, mind, and fortune. Miss Sedgwick presents a sympathetic portrait of a person belonging to an old city family and shows her kindly disposed towards former neighbors who have wealth but who lack some of the qualities thought necessary for social acceptance. Mrs. Mowatt makes clear her belief that family tradition is not so important as culture and integrity of conduct. Howells is critical of city persons of breeding and social prominence for their lack of hospitality and general indifference towards those whom they regard as inferiors. He is also keen enough to note certain fundamental deficiencies in their relations one with the other which prevent absolute harmony of home-life. Crawford finds more serious faults in the lives of the one family group in whom he is greatly interested. Warner finds moneyed classes associating on equal terms with persons of breeding and thinks nothing of it: but with Edgar Fawcett these two classes are continually at logger-heads and he satirizes both. Our novelists thus are not agreed that social prestige in the city should be restricted to those belonging to old city families. The latter are strongly criticized by some of these writers; but by others they are shown living on equal and peaceful terms with the newly-rich class.

The *nouveau riche* are also severely condemned and satirized as intruders, particularly by Cooper, Mrs. Otis, Fawcett, and Mrs. Harrison. Howells is more discriminating: in Silas Lapham he presents a sympathetic illustration of that class, while in Dryfoos he creates one who arouses nothing but disfavor.

Several authors wrote vividly of persons whose lives were controlled by passion for social acceptance. Mrs. Kirk's Margaret Kent is an excellent instance; in her case, success came by reason of cleverness and pleasing personality. Robert Grant shows, in the career of Flossy Williams, that such ambition may lead to the use of methods far from commendable.

As to the literary quality of the contributions to the social life of the city, one is forced to conclude that the best results were obtained by the later writers, those of the eighties and nineties. This was to be expected, since the greatest contrasts came in those decades. The novelists were then beginning to take notice of the rise into prominence of a new class who obtained leadership in the city by means of achievement and not by birth. Its emergence brought new problems and caused writers to re-estimate the whole system. In the case of the writers of the seventies, the realignment of forces was too close at hand to be easily and conveniently adapted into fiction; but in the last two decades of the century there was just the proper amount of perspective for the authors to appreciate the problem at its real value. Consequently, almost all of them represented the social situation as a vital part of the city novel. That only a few novels were entirely social in nature is explained by the fact that, as usual, the authors chose to divide their attention among the many and varying interests that the city so readily provided for them. Especially noteworthy for adherence to social questions and for power in presentation of them were the following novels: *The Rise of Silas Lapham; A Hazard of New Fortunes; April Hopes; The Story of Margaret Kent; Katharine Lauderdale; The Ralstons;* and *Unleavened Bread.* These novels are also to be praised for the entertaining style in which they are written, for the reality with which the characters are developed, and for the general background of truth with which the social situations are surrounded.

Works cited in this chapter by Howells, Crawford, Warner, and Mitchell are particularly to be commended for their accurate portraiture of members of the so-called aristocratic groups which are so influential in American cities. One may make excellent selections from these novels of life-like personages to represent these groups. One could include in this list the Coreys, Bellinghams, Pasmers, and Maverings from the novels of Howells, the Lauderdales from Crawford, the Hendersons from Warner, and Dr. North and his friends from Mitchell. All of these are splendid examples of persons of wealth and social distinction and were probably drawn from real life. It was thought necessary to make this special comment upon them because a number of other novelists mentioned in this same chapter were considerably less successful in their efforts to create adequate representatives of this class. This was true of Cooper in his *Home as Found;* of Mrs. Stowe in *My Wife and I* and *We and Our Neighbors;* of Henry James in *Washington Square,* and of Edgar Fawcett in *Olivia Delaplaine* and *A Gentleman of Leisure.* In these novels the aristocratic characters are artificial and uninteresting and distinctly failures in so far as they are supposed to represent real persons. It is a relief, therefore, to be able to point to the excellence of the characterizations found in the works of Howells, Mitchell, Crawford, and Warner.

CHAPTER V

The Literary and Artistic Life of the City

Men of letters, journalists, artists, and musicians found in the city the greatest possibilities for development of their abilities, and they found there also congenial fellow-workers with whom they could profitably associate. Their struggles with the city environment have already been considered, and in this chapter attention will be directed to their moments of leisure and recreation. In contrast with the coteries noted in the previous chapter, membership in this one is guaranteed by neither money nor birth. The only certain method of entrance is through possession of literary, artistic, or musical talent or of sympathy with those talents.

Our novelists of urban life have shown keen interest in this group. Their enthusiasm for it is reflected in pleasant interludes in their novels describing some of its happy meetings. For the reader seeking to picture the literary and artistic scene the interludes provide invaluable assistance since they bring him detailed descriptions of individual poets, novelists, newspaper men, artists, and musicians, whom he sees at their ease enjoying brief relaxation from their tasks. For the lover of literature, the interludes may occasionally provide a peculiar and indefinable charm not to be obtained from the representation of more pretentious but less spontaneous assemblies.

An early example of this interest is found in Cooper's *Home as Found*, where the author satirically describes an evening of literature at Mrs. Legend's drawing-room. By his ridicule he makes it almost a farce. His aim was to expose the absurdities of the intellectual life fostered by the "uninstructed taste" of the *nouveau riche* in the New York of the thirties. It was a cosmopolitan affair at which "nearly all the wits, writers, artists, and literati" of the city were present. The humor of the occasion (a heavy sort of humor it is) is provided by the circumstance that the hardy sea captain Turck is mistakenly supposed to be the "Hon. and Rev. Mr. Turck", an English clergyman who had come to New York to study its social life in preparation for writing a book on American character. Literature, as represented by the assemblage at Mrs. Legend's, was rallying to the defence of the city's culture. When Captain Turck made his entrance into the drawing-room, his appearance was well adapted to his supposed character. His hair, nearly as white as snow, gave him the needed dignity of age. "The hale, fresh, red of his features, which was in truth the result of exposure, might very well pass for the tint of port," and his tread, which had always a little of the quarter-deck swing about it, might quite easily be mistaken by a tyro, for the human frame staggering under a load of learning."* When he began to smoke a cigar, the literati at once began to debate whether or not smoking was genteel in England and mentally searched into contemporary English fiction for an answer. The captain's contribution to the discussion—a statement that the English clergy used cigars in their pulpits—and his own indulgence in the habit seemed to decide the question. Some of his admirers then agreed that it was a good custom, for in their minds any custom that was sanctioned by the English was worthy of their acceptance. Various problems of English literature were expounded to Turck and received non-committal replies from him, which, to his deluded audience seemed pearls of wisdom. The whole episode is rather heavily handled by Cooper, who seemed to lack the lightness of touch that such a situation demanded. His attitude towards the social climbers of New York city was probably too contemptuous to permit him to compose a clever satire of them. He made their actions so stupid and so ridiculous that the reader cannot appreciate his purpose.

Bayard Taylor was more deeply interested in the literary-artistic New York than was Cooper and consequently his reports of it are more convincing. Literary and musical temperaments are shown in pleasing harmony in John Godfrey and Swansford. The friendship of these two young men provides one of the charms of *John Godfrey's Fortunes*. It is a fortunate companionship, for without it each would have been very lonely at Mrs.

---

*Cooper, J. Fenimore—"Home as Found", Phila., 1838, v. 1, 97.

Very's boarding-house where they lodge. There are no other congenial souls to attract them. At the dinner table the talk of the other boarders consists mainly of commercial topics or just gossip. Godfrey and his musical friend, glad to escape to their rooms, derive considerable enjoyment there from composing verses and songs.

A party to which all the boarders are invited is cleverly described by Taylor without the use of the satire or exaggeration that marred Cooper's literary evening in *Home as Found.* One feels that the author's presentation is an accurate picture of such a party and that he may be drawing upon his own experience for it, for he himself lived for a time in New York as a young man. The entertainment on this occasion is not entirely pleasing to Swansford, for, after singing one of his own songs, he is distressed at being compelled to listen to the singing of a number of popular sentimental ballads. On return to his room he vents his wrath upon the composers of such trivialities by producing a clever burlesque of them, using the honeyed verses that Godfrey's facile pen provided. This was sold the next day for $75.

Godfrey's other acquaintances, with whom he spends hilarious evenings at the Cave of Trophonius, are not as upright and conscientious as Swansford. They are Bohemians who, like him, pursue literature for a living, but in their periods of recreation seem more like rowdies than literary workers.

Taylor's affection for the literary life led him to devote most of his novel to it. It remains till the present day a worthy example of the novel with literary and artistic background and was especially significant among the novels of its own time for the reality of its picture of the literary scene in New York city.

Mrs. Rebecca H. Davis did not give as much attention to literary life in *Earthen Pitchers* (1874)* but the literary soirée which she depicts there has some of the virtues of Taylor's literary scenes in its sincerity and evident sympathy with literary and artistic people. What satire is present is made subordinate to good humor, and there is no repetition of Cooper's heavy absurdities. As Mrs. Davis was thoroughly familiar with the

---

*Scribner's Monthly, 1873-4.

intellectual life of Philadelphia, where she lived after her marriage, it is not surprising that the literary meeting should be placed in that city. Again it is a woman who is the sponsor—a Miss Derby—who is not a member of exclusive Quaker social circles, since she lives north of Market Street. Her particular task is the writing of book reviews and a woman's column, but she is known better among her Bohemian associates for her Saturday evening receptions. At one of these she has as a special attraction an exhibition of pictures brought there for a private viewing, and for possible sale. There is little action at the affair, and its value lies in the description of the guests. One of them, a publisher by the name of John Shively, reminds the reader of Theodore Fay's character Earnest, who talked with the royalty "and intelligentsia of England and France." Shively boasts of personal meetings with the Earl of Dundas, the Prince of Wales, and a Russian prince. Unlike Earnest, he does not become infatuated with England. There are the usual number of artists and writers, described with a reality untouched by idealism. Indeed, a cousin of Miss Derby's is so disappointed at his first meeting with intellectual celebrities that he inquires: "Was this genius?" In answer to his own question he complains that their talk "sounded to him like gossip, smelling rankly of paint and ink." Miss Derby married Niel Goddard, a painter who is endowed with the short-comings generally ascribed to the artistic temperament. His special caprice is indulgence in platonic friendships for other women, which his wife regards with a philosophical eye and excuses on the ground that they are only marks of the "frailties of genius". She herself was only too glad to have escaped from her former newspaper life in the city, an existence which she had once denounced as a "wretched sham" and her own soirées as nothing but "tasteless tea" and "chaffy toast" and "huckster notions of art and authorship."

Edgar Fawcett is another author who interpolates a literary evening into the course of his narrative. In *A Gentleman of Leisure* there is a humorous description of such an affair held in the parlors of Mrs. Lucretia Bateson Bangs. At this fashionable city home gather a number of oddities. Among them are (1) a woman journalist from the Green Mountains who is distinguished principally for her lack of education and enjoys the startling name of Mrs. Eleanor Polhemus Brown; (2) Large, a coming poet who writes democratic chants about boundless prairies and brotherly love and the grand coming amelioration of humanity, jumbles together Carlyle and Emerson in a wild parody, discards rhyme, and metre and insults art; and (3) the antithesis of Large and his sworn enemy — the dilettante T. Rochester Hilliard who is a fervent advocate of art for art's sake, adores the past as much as Large detests it, and shrinks from science and modern progress. One may find in Hilliard a suggestion of the opposition to the new era in American literature which Walt Whitman had advocated ten years before in his Democratic Vistas. There he had called for a literature of the people and "a poetry that is bold, modern . . . and that must in no respect ignore science or the modern, but inspire itself with science and the modern" and "must bend its vision toward the future, more than the past."* Whitman might therefore be identified with Large† since he had opposed just the things which Large was said to have opposed, namely, American literature's shrinking away from science and the modern, and the glance towards the past, instead of the future.

Since there is no further mention of these oddities in the novel, the reader must believe that they were included by the author merely because he thought them an essential part of the complete city scene which he was endeavoring to draw. The value of the scene, therefore, lies in its suggestion of the literary fashions which were in control in New York at the time of writing. Humor is present to some extent, but satire is the prevailing tone.

In *A Modern Instance* Howells pictures a literary meeting lacking the diversified character of those just described. It was a specialized group—a club composed entirely of New York's leading newspaper men. Bartley Hubbard, visiting it for the first time, was impressed with the enthusiasm and loyalty of the

---

*See "The Prose Works of Walt Whitman, Phila., David McKay, 245-6.

†A reviewer in the Literary World (vol. xii, 258, July 30, 1881) sees in Large "an obvious caricature of Mr. George Edgar Montgomery, whose poetry, like Wagner's music, is 'of the future'."

men to their chosen profession. Gathered at an old-fashioned hotel were editors, reporters and feature writers who met about a dinner table, partook of a rather poor meal but enjoyed themselves with informal talks. The members were mostly young men who were lured into journalism by the prospect of excitement and adventure despite low salaries. A few older men were there too—proud of their vocation even though recent radical changes in it had left them somewhat superannuated. Howells may be recalling his own early newspaper days when he writes that to each of the journalists there assembled his particular newspaper was regarded as something to serve day and night, and that it was necessary to "merge himself in its glory, and to live in its triumphs without personal recognition from the public."* He also declares that "none . . . who have ever known it, can wholly forget the generous rage with which journalism inspires its followers."* The reader does not, however, find much expression of this rage in Howells. For vivid touches of city newspaper life one must turn to the short stories of Richard Harding Davis or Jesse Lynch Williams. The short story, by its brevity and conciseness, seems on the whole more adapted to the tale of newspaper adventures than does the longer narrative.

William H. Bishop devotes a separate chapter of *The House of a Merchant Prince* to an "Evening in Literary Society", thus following the practice of Cooper, Mrs. Davis, and Edgar Fawcett in making the city's literary life an isolated event. Celebrities are described one after the other in catalogue fashion, and scraps of their conversations are introduced to explain their characters, but the whole lacks continuity. Satire is plentifully in evidence; the author is no doubt drawing upon his own experience with such meetings and may even have intended some of the personages to represent real men and women of New York's Bohemia, as Fawcett did. During the evening an entertainment, partly musical, partly histrionic, is provided by the hostess. Several recitations are given—one by a tragic actress who reads from Mrs. Browning—and verses are read by several rising poets who had come well prepared with manuscripts in their inside pockets.

---

*A Modern Instance, 196-197.

To show the cosmopolitan character of the assembly, one has but to name some of those present: a publisher; a South American traveller; Ringrose, the poet; Professor Brown whose speciality was the popularization of science; a Shakespearean entertainer; an historian; an elderly journalist; a painter; several actresses; a woman who wrote "matter of small importance with a spiteful tang"; and Count Altamont who posed as a traveler, poet, and amateur in all the fine arts and was popular with the female sex. The Western flavor, which was generally felt essential for these occasions, was supplied by an Indian boy in full feathers and deer-skin.

Bishop was attempting in this novel to give the reader a full picture of New York life, and for this purpose wrote episodes descriptive of the Sunday parade on Fifth Avenue after church, a millionaire's new home and a house-warming there; a dinner to a celebrity; and the life of typical city "swells". The literary society also occupies his attention temporarily. Its meeting is not particularly entertaining as the author has described it, but one can say in its favor that it helps to identify the particular literary and artistic fashions that were prevailing at the time. In this respect it is more valuable than Fawcett's literary evening in *A Gentleman of Leisure* since it presents a more complete report.

In two novels by Arlo Bates one may find the artistic life of the city occupying a position of prominence and not a subordinate one as in many of the previous novels noted. *The Pagans* (1884) and *The Philistines* (1888) deal with the contest in Boston's world of art between originality and conventionality, the Pagans representing the former and the Philistines the latter. More explicitly, the Pagans represented the protest of the artistic soul against sham. They stood for absolute sincerity in art, life, manners, and morals. In their minds Philistinism denoted imitation and subservience to authority, for which they had no tolerance. The struggle is centered in the person of Arthur Fenton, a painter with an erratic character in which extravagance, selfishness, cynicism, and love of splendor and ease predominate. By marriage with the daughter of the leader of the Philistines, he hopes to make peace with that group, but his friends disapprove of his turning away from them and continue their antagonism to the Philistines. His former strict standards of art gradually deteriorate as he concentrates on doing work that will bring him in money, regardless of its artistic worth. With his abandonment of Pagan principles that group of sturdy followers of high art disband. The plot of the novel is not a strong one; but it shows the usual jealousies, irregular love affairs, and misconduct of artist models that one generally finds in the fiction reporting the life of artist colonies of a large city. The author's satire is directed against committees which select sculptors to execute works of art for city beautiful projects. Such a committee as described by him contains three members, appointed by City Hall. One is an example of the best type of American gentleman; another is a rich art patron—a Philistine; and the third knows nothing whatever about art but hopes by serving on the committee to build up a reputation as a connoisseur. There is a great deal of inside influence exerted; and their final selection, the young, untried Orlan Stanton, proves an unfortunate one, for his statue when completed and exhibited in his studio is recognized and exposed by critics as a design stolen from a statuette in the Vatican.

In his treatment of Browning clubs, the wit of the novelist is seen to its best advantage. He declares that a genuine, serious Boston Browning Club is as deliciously droll as any form of entertainment ever devised. The meetings, held in splendidly furnished homes, are attended mostly by women who regard Browning's poems with such awe and veneration that they converse together in subdued tones. The readings of the poems may seem dull to the uninitiated, and to the "elderly and corpulent devotees who listen only with the spiritual ear (slumber)". In the discussions that follow the readings the principle seems to be that "a poem by Robert Browning is a sort of prize enigma, of which the solution is to be reached rather by wild and daring guessing than by any commonplace process of reasoning."* The Browningite is "deeply aware that if the poet seems to say one thing, this is proof indisputable that another is intended. To

*Bates, Arlo—"These Philistines", Boston, 1888, 31.

take a work in a straightforward fashion would at once rob the
Browning Club of all excuse for existence. . . . When all else
fails, moreover, the club can always fall back upon allegory. . . .
Let a poem be considered an allegory, and there is no limit to the
changes which may be rung upon it."* At the meeting partic-
ularized in the novel the masculine element seems to be unusually
prominent. Thus a man does the reading for the day (*Bishop
Blougram's Apology*), and several men join in the discussion,
notably Arthur Fenton and an Episcopalian rector. Fenton had
not been listening to the poem, the reading of which had con-
sumed more than an hour, but had amused himself with drawing
caricatures of the company. When suddenly called upon for
comments he readily says a few words which are quite as intelligent as the remarks of others who have been deeply attentive.
A warm argument between him and the rector is narrowly averted
when Arthur's wife, who is deeply religious, sides with the minister. The affair is hardly to be dignified with the adjective
"literary", though no doubt it was typical of the meetings of many
other such organizations in the Boston of the late eighties.

Arlo Bates' novels are important for their keen analysis of the
artistic temperament. There are several examples of this, the
best of which is Arthur Fenton whose unreliability inevitably
invites comparison with that of Angus Beaton in Howells'
A Hazard of New Fortunes. Fenton is not quite as finished a
portrait as Beaton, but when he and his fellow artists are assembled together, one may obtain a more comprehensive picture
of the city's artistic world than is to be found in Howells' works.
Bates differs decidedly from Howells in the fact that he does not
hesitate to emphasize the irregularities of artist life, which Howells
avoids except in Beaton. His style is noteworthy for bitter satire
and for its frequent use of the epigram, somewhat in the manner
of Henry James. Some of his best work is found in the description of social, intellectual gatherings like the meeting of the
Browning Society which has already received comment. His
improvement upon the efforts of writers like Fawcett and Bishop
in dealing with such affairs is that he makes his principal char-

---

*ibid., 31-2.

acters take an active part therein. In this manner the reader is induced to take more real interest in them. Also he concentrates his attention upon the activities of the meeting which he makes humorously attractive, while Fawcett and Bishop seem content to devote their time to naming one after another the persons who are present.

In that particular division of city life treated by Bates, appreciation of literature and art was little more than a fad. In some of the foreign sections of a large city one may find that literature, music, and art play a more vital part in the lives of the people. There one may discover real Bohemians living in conditions bordering closely upon poverty, but enjoying that happiness which true devotion to the aesthetic life invariably brings. At least two of the romances of Henry Harland owe their charm to a sympathetic portrayal of just such life. Covering a small range, they introduce few characters, and in this manner achieve a nearer approach to unity than is usually found in the city novel. *As It Was Written* (1885) describes the life of musical enthusiasts. The romance between Ernest Neuman, Jewish novelist and Veronica, a talented soprano, is strengthened by their devotion to the compositions of the old masters. Veronica's father is also a musician and a composer, who, like Swansford in *John Godfrey's Fortunes* was at work upon what was intended to be "an epoch-making symphony." The three often spend very congenial evenings with their music, but the reader soon suspects that such Elysian happiness cannot long persist, and he is not surprised therefore when there is a tragic interlude culminating in the strange death of Veronica. Music continues its all-important role in the story, for after an interval Ernest is shown leading another pleasant Bohemian life in bachelor quarters with a newly-found chum, the poet Daniel Merivale, who unlike most young poets in New York, seems plentifully supplied with money so that he can engage Ernest as his private secretary to write poems from his dictation. One must not, of course, expect to find realism in the works of Harland; the pictures of city life which he provides are idealistic. Neuman and Merivale develop into warm friends. Their chief enjoyments are with intellectual matters; the reading together of poets like Browning and Rossetti;

visiting picture galleries and playing violin duets. Happiness again becomes excessive and as a compensation the author completes his tale with a fantastic disclosure of Ernest's guilt in killing his sweetheart. This is made through his playing on the violin of a long and weird composition which startles both himself and Merivale. They search but cannot find the original for the music; then determine to transcribe it into musical notations. While Ernest is doing this, he unconsciously writes not only musical characters but also a complete written report of the circumstances preceding his murder of Veronica. While such a situation approximates 'the impossible and incredible, it is strictly in accordance with his usual utter absorption in his music when playing the violin, for on such occasions he generally lapses into semi-consciousness and permits another spirit, as it were, to control his instrument.

As It Was Written has an intensely interesting plot and is the best of his stories laid in New York city. *Mrs. Peixada* (1886) presented more idealistic musical scenes in New York's world of Bohemia, but was not as successful as the former. The hero and heroine become acquainted as a result of the latter's exquisite singing of classical songs by Schubert and Chopin, but the musical atmosphere is not long sustained in this novel. It soon yields to legal problems connected with a murder case but not before Harland has interpolated a satirical account of a meeting of Wagnerites, where devotees of that much maligned composer defend their idol and incidentally throw up their hands with horror at mention of the few occasions when he seemed to fall from grace by insertion of melody in his compositions. Of the "Pilgrim's Chorus" in Tannhauser, they declare that it was unfortunate that Wagner "could have let himself down to anything so trivial."* And, of course, they do not approve of the beautiful melodies of Schubert whose songs were great favorites with the heroine of the story.

Interest in the poems of Robert Browning is suggested in this

*Mrs. Kirk in *Queen Money* (1888) also refers to the contemporary musical tastes. She depicts an amusing scene in which two elderly men openly opposed to Wagner, attend a performance of Die Walkure and are secretly pleased with the modernity of the music, but are unwilling to acknowledge it because of their oft-repeated preference for Beethoven.

novel, and it is less analytical than the sleuth-like investigations of the Browning Club described by Bates. It is reflected in the conversation of the hero of the story and in Mrs. Peixada's fondness for *The Ring and the Book,* which she lends him to read, telling him that she loves it almost as if it were a human being. The two often sit in Central Park reading from their favorite and other well-known authors.

The superiority of *As It Was Written* to *Mrs. Peixada* is explained by the fact that its Bohemianism is well-sustained and charmingly described throughout the whole novel. In *Mrs. Peixada* it is not so significant, and the novel has value for this study only because of its casual references to musical controversies of the day and to the fondness for Browning among intellectual and artistic people.

In *A Little Upstart* by William H. Rideing (1885) one may find sketches of two novelists—a man who wrote introspective studies of the human mind which were not at all popular, and a country girl from Vermont who came to Boston and scored one success with a novel taken from her own intimate diary. They are writers who are typical of their time, but most originality is found in the character of Mrs. Amelia Bailey Ames who sets for herself the task of acting as patron and sponsor for Boston literary celebrities. She herself had written sobbing and lovesick verses, a few of which were published at the expense of her husband, under the title, "With Bitter Tears Bedewed and Other Poems." These gave her some of the notoriety that she desired, for she was interested in obtaining recognition by the city's well-established families, an ambition she hoped to realize by the Sunday literary evenings held in her own home. There one meets individuals who are as odd as those who attended the gatherings described by Cooper, Fawcett, and Bishop. Among them is a Western poet, Coronado Romero, called "Our Western Byron." The fact that he is stated to be the author of *Songs of the Sacramento* and *Ballads of the Boulders,* and that he wears a blue flannel shirt and high boots and carries a six shooter and bowie knife would suggest that Romero is intended for a caricature of the eccentric Joaquin Miller.

One finds in Rideing's book also some indication of the vogue

which a new novelist enjoys in the city. Miriam Belknap is introduced into Boston intellectual circles by Mrs. Ames and becomes
acquainted with some well-known families, but many of them
later turn against her on account of the crude behavior of her
sponsor. For a time she attends frequently at Boston's many
public lectures, private views of pictures, spiritual séances, plays,
receptions, and symphony concerts. The author's comments upon
these affairs offer illuminating side-lights on their real nature.
Miriam is taken to London—the Mecca of the American social
pretenders of the time—and there Mrs. Ames obtains a court
presentation for her. But when her second novel proves to be
a total failure, she has to return to New York by herself and
live in temporary obscurity and poverty until accidentally discovered by her husband from whom she had been estranged.
Rideing's novel is almost entirely social and literary in its emphasis, and is not a great work of art but is of value for its
accurate portrayal of the habits of literary men and women of
Boston and of their close relation with the social life of the city.

The artistic temperament, eccentricities of which have been
seen in Arthur Fenton as created by Arlo Bates, is again critically
analyzed in the person of Angus Beaton in *A Hazard of New
Fortunes*. By occupation an artist and syndicate writer on art
subjects, Beaton is notoriously untrustworthy in his social obliga-
tions. A few illustrations will show this. One of his acquaintances,
a young woman by the name of Alma Leighton, has come with
her mother to New York to study art principally at his instiga-
tion, but he neglects to call upon her for a long time after her
arrival there. Alma explains his lack of sociability by saying
that "artists never do anything like other people." Howells en-
larges upon his unreliability by stating that he thinks himself
privileged to break an engagement or fail to keep an appointment
whenever his convenience seems to demand such conduct. At
the time of making his promises he fully intends to keep them,
and his failure to do so is owing to his fickleness. While he loses
some friends by his actions, most people understand his oddities
and are patient with them. Beaton seems incapable of serious
courtship of any girl. Christine Dryfoos has attracted him by
her beauty and wildness of disposition that always makes him

feel when he is with her as if he is "holding a leopardess in leash." But he does not love her and therefore when he is dismissed from the Dryfoos home because he will not admit any serious intention in coming to see Christine, he is not greatly disturbed. He is more bothered when Alma, whom he has always loved in spite of his indifferent treatment of her, finally rejects his advances. Christine, too, refuses to forgive him when he is again permitted to resume his visits, for she sees that he has no regard for her. Therefore, in the end, Beaton's social relations in the city are shown to be decidedly insecure, though in his artistic work he has made quite satisfactory progress. The reader finds him as subtle as most of Howells' characters through the equal distribution of good and evil qualities. His particular value in a review of artistic life is that he represents a vivid portrayal of an artist unable to harmonize his temperament with the various personalities whom he meets in the normal courses of his city life.

The Coast of Bohemia (1893) is concerned principally with the life of New York's art students. One finds here pictures/of the serious efforts of young people to learn the basic principles of painting at the Synthesis of Art Studies (the Art Students' League of New York) and also a representation of their lighter moments devoted to recreation. One meets here the country girl Cornelia Saunders who has come to New York with high expectation of developing her talents as a painter; one meets too a girl from a wealthy home—Charmian Maybough, and one sees her own private studio located in the attic of her mother's luxuriously-furnished rooms. The studio is littered with oil and charcoal sketches, an easel, and a table loaded with palettes and brushes. On the floor is a tiger skin, sprawled in front of the fire-place. Here the two girls are able to enjoy many moments of pseudo-Bohemian existence. Cornelia progresses gradually with her painting and, of course, has a romance with one of the greatest painters in the city. At the close of the novel is found an entertaining description of an exhibition of art work and a masquerade dance given by the Synthesis students; and there is a slight reference to a Bohemian dinner given in honor of Ludlow and Cornelia by Charmian who complains afterwards that the affair was not strictly Bohemian since the ladies did not remain with

the men after the meal and smoke cigarettes. Howells is more
lenient with the artistic temperament in this novel than he was in
the case of Angus Beaton, and his treatment of artists, both
masculine and feminine, is on the whole an optimistic one. He
refused to introduce scandal into the lives of artists. The Bohemian life was certainly not always as mild and uneventful and
devoid of escapades as he painted it, but since he was not at all
in sympathy with the wilder features of that life, one must not
complain because he did not exhibit them in this novel. The book
itself has some amusing moments, but looking at it from the
standpoint of the struggle for success in art on the part of a newcomer to the metropolitan centre, the reader cannot help feeling
that the expectations aroused at its beginning, are not fulfilled,
for Cornelia is soon side-tracked from adherence to her ambitions
by her love for Ludlow.

The artist in Crawford's Lauderdale novels, Walter Crowdie,
is a man well-versed in city customs. He is polite and sociable,
but rather weak. To some he is repulsive for reasons which
they cannot analyze. Katharine Lauderdale thinks of him as
like "some strange tropical fruit gone bad at the core." His
wife, Hester, is intensely in love with him and absurdly jealous
of any woman to whom he appears to show any marked attention.
Combined with his ability as a painter is another talent, that of
the singer. At informal social functions he is able to entertain
quite acceptably with his songs, but there, as always, Hester is
anxiously on the watch. All his songs must have her as his
only inspiration; and when she discovers that he sang on one
occasion directly for Katharine, she scolds him severely. To her
seems to have been transferred a large portion of artistic temperament. In Crowdie's studio one may find many evidences of his
fondness for the exotic in the barbaric wealth of rich Eastern
carpets, stuffs, and embroideries draped about the walls and huge
divans.

The companionship of Crowdie and Paul Griggs, cosmopolitan
novelist, forms another touch of the unusual and even mysterious,
for they were boon companions in their apprenticeship days in the
Latin Quarter of Paris, and know facts about each other of which
others do not suspect. The part taken by Griggs in the conver-

sations of the city's social groups to which he is admitted is an important one. He is particularly adept in expressing his opinions. They are not all conservative but often are unconventional, owing to his familiarity with foreign habits and customs acquired in many years of travel. In some respects, he is a strong contrast to that other novelist creation of Crawford's—George Wood —who also lived in New York. Wood was not a fluent talker like Griggs, nor as much the man of the world as Griggs. His works were a product of inspirational moments when he was carried away from his ordinary, commonplace self into a man of genius and imagination. Griggs, on the other hand, wrote, one may believe, not so much from inspiration as from his wide experience. One thinks at once of Shelley Ray's literary friend, Kane, with whom Ray spent profitable hours, but whose book was declared by Brandreth, the publisher, to be much less interesting than the man himself. This might also be said of Griggs, for the reader is much more entertained by listening to his talk than he could possibly be by hearing of his activities as a writer of fiction. Both Crowdie and Griggs are well-drawn characters. Each has a distinct individuality. Crowdie, like Angus Beaton and Arthur Fenton, is not especially pleasing in his actions. Griggs is more pleasing and more interesting on account of the originality of his opinions and his brilliance in expressing them. The close companionship of these two has some resemblance to the friendship between Godfrey and Swansford, for in both there is union of aesthetic natures. Crawford's characters are, of course, older men and their friendship had its origin in Bohemian life together in Europe, while Taylor's characters formed their friendship in New York City.

The artist life pictured in Stephen Crane's *The Third Violet* (1897) is in great contrast with that depicted by Bates, Howells, and Crawford. In none of the latter is the reader impressed with the harsh features of that life. Instead he sees its comfortable side. Crane, on the other hand, emphasizes the fact that artists living in a great city must struggle for mere existence. In sketching the career of four young artists in New York he shows them dwelling in a small room in an old begrimed building placed between two large business structures. Here they eat, sleep, and work. Billie Hawker, who has more talent and hence a little more money, has a larger studio adjoining theirs. All are bachelors and are generally out of money. The one who has any at all is expected to share it with the others so as to provide a common fund with which to buy food, or pay the month's rent.

The comfortable kind of artist life is likewise suggested by the author when he has Hawker's rich friend, Miss Fanhall, tell of her experience with another artist acquaintance at a studio-tea. She describes his "dearest little Japanese servants," the tea cups from Algiers and Turkey, and the harmonious coloring of the studio furnishings. In her opinion the man must have led a "lazy, beautiful life . . . lounging in such a studio, smoking monogrammed cigarettes, and remarking how badly all the other men painted."* Hawker explains to her that such indolence gives an incorrect impression of an artist's life, and proceeds to relate his own experience. He was compelled, he states, to earn more than half the money needed for his education, part of which was obtained in Paris. Then after returning to New York he had a long period of discouraging and unsuccessful effort before he could earn a fair income.

The comradery of Bohemian life is ably described in this novel. A model, Florinda, is an intimate associate of the artists and is a guest at their celebrations where they partake of sphagetti, wine, and potato salad. She helps to carry through the slight plot, for she had once been Billie Hawker's favorite until he met the more attractive girl from the city's fashionable circles. His abandonment of her arouses her jealousy, but in the end she has to endure the prospect of seeing herself permanently supplanted. The story progresses by means of short, choppy conversations, most of which are insignificant, though supposed to be actual reproductions of the talk of real persons. The value of the novel is not therefore in its workmanship but rather in its portrayal of Bohemian life in the large city from the viewpoint of those for whom it is an uncompromising struggle for existence. In this struggle the cheerfulness and good-nature of the artists are characteristics especially noted by the author.

---

*Crane, Stephen—"The Third Violet", New York, 1897, 180.

Certain episodes in Matthews' *A Confident To-morrow* reveal the social side of Frank Sartain's literary career. That young man is not as good an illustration of the Bohemian as the artists of the Crane novel primarily because of his extreme bashfulness —a fault which he never seems able to overcome. More nearly resembling true Bohemians are some of Sartain's acquaintances, among whom is Adams, a young artist who had lived for two years in the Parisian Latin Quarter. He had become a great lover of New York; while walking with Sartain on Fifth Avenue he exclaims upon its beauty and praises cities in general, saying, "A great city is the final achievement" of the nineteenth century and its "perfect flower". Adams supplies a great deal of the enthusiasm that one finds lacking in Sartain's nature. Matthews' own love of New York and his familiarity with its Bohemian life are evidenced by his inclusion in this novel of a scene laid in one of the city's Italian restaurants known as "The Fried Cat." Here Adams and Sartain dine and Adams entertains with an account of his life in Paris, after which two others are admitted to the table—two poets well known to Sartain by reputation but whom he had never met. One of them, Jerry Quinn, writes Irish dialect verse but is not himself Irish. The other, Clarence Shields, writes light, airy lyrics. The scene is short and entirely too short, so that the reader may well believe that Sartain's judgment is exaggerated when he declares that it was his first introduction into "the New York circle which most closely corresponded to that in Paris celebrated by Henry Murger."* Matthews no doubt had a truly Bohemian gathering pictured in his mind, but he did not develop it sufficiently in this scene. This is one of the faults of his novels—that, although he is inspired by intense affection for New York life, he cannot always make an adequate transfer of his affection into print. Incidents in this novel, as in this case, are often too sketchy. The conversations of his characters some-times err in the opposite way, namely, that they contain more material than the reader can conveniently assimilate at one time. Too much is implied in what they say, and there is not enough of simple, direct statement. His thorough knowledge of the literary

---

*Matthews, Brander—"A Confident To-Morrow", New York, 1900, 147.

and social phases of New York life must not, however, be forgotten, and for this alone his novels are worthy of careful reading.

In this review of urban literary and artistic life, one notes the frequent recurrence of scenes depicting literary soirées, held usually in the city's fashionable homes. The authors are often satirical in their attitude towards them. Those who attend are the oddities of this kind of city life. In several of them direct references to contemporary personages may be traced. They were generally placed in isolated positions in the novels where they had little or no connection with the plot development. Their sponsors, chiefly women, were motivated by social ambition, hoping to attract attention to themselves and secure acceptance into city homes hitherto denied to them. Exception to this tendency may be seen in Miss Derby's receptions in *Earthen Pitchers,* where the motive appears to be more unselfish and closely approximates a sincere concern for the intellectual development of her acquaintances. The Browning Society meetings likewise were intended for intellectual exercise, but according to Arlo Bates, they were rather misguided affairs that failed of their original purpose, since they obscured the great poet's verses more often than they clarified them.

Informal musical and literary meetings, composed of smaller groups than the soirées, were productive of more real appreciation. Here one finds the best presentation of the aesthetic life as lived in the large city. The episodic method again is often used as in the description of the soirées, but there are more exceptions to the rule, notably in the works of Henry Harland. Musical gatherings are prominent and it is significant that the best of the foreign composers are called upon to provide the compositions played or sung. One often finds in these gatherings a predominance of foreigners representing many different nations, but the novelists were not entirely unpatriotic, for one finds good native musicians, particularly those of the Jewish faith. The music of Wagner provided occasion for several serio-comic situations, as it often did in real life during the eighties and nineties when the city musical world was stirred to its very foundations by the introduction of Wagner's music dramas. In the realm of literature, Robert Browning seemed to attract a great deal of attention from city lovers of poetry if one is to accept the word of the contemporary novelist. Not only did organized clubs discuss his thought-provoking poems, but they were also read and debated by friends in private homes and by lovers on Park benches. The vogue for Browning in the latter part of the period was then just as important in city life as the vogue for Wagner.

Of the individuals met in this review, it would seem that the artists suffered most harshly at the hands of their creators. As one glances down the list, one finds few favorable treatments of them. Niel Goddard, Arthur Fenton, Angus Beaton, and Walter Crowdie all had more or less serious flaws in their characters. The only absolutely upright artist creations were Walter Ludlow in *The Coast of Bohemia,* Billie Hawker in *The Third Violet,* and Adams, a minor figure, in *A Confident To-morrow.* Westover, who was considered in connection with Jeff Durgin in a previous chapter, may also be added to the list. The city novelists and journalists received kinder and more sympathetic consideration in that they were shown to be less erratic in social behavior than the artists. Bartley Hubbard is, of course, an exception, for his irregularity of conduct was about on a par with that of Beaton. The poets were slighted, being few in number and minor characters. John Godfrey may be counted among them, but his verse writing after removal to the city was almost abandoned for the more lucrative field of journalism. Merivale in *As It Was Written* is a sympathetic character but as a poet he resembles the dilettante. The writing of verses was not unusually associated by our novelists with life in a large, crowded city. Very probably they believed that poetical inspiration was more easily obtained in the seclusion of rural life.

The novelistic treatment of the literary and artistic life of the city yields some pleasing scenes, though there are comparatively few novels that maintain a continuous attention to it. Henry Harland's touch seems to be the lightest and most attractive. Bayard Taylor has some excellent scenes giving vivid flashes of this life. Howells has one excellent creation—a typical artist— in Beaton, but *The Coast of Bohemia* is good only for scattered amusing incidents, and *The World of Chance* would have been a better treatment of literary life if it had not been side-tracked so often into a consideration of industrial and economic problems. Arlo Bates' pictures of artists in Boston are rather flippant in tone.   Crawford is more unaffected and does not exaggerate or over-stress the irregularities of artist life in the city. Stephen Crane's one work dealing with artists in the city is worthy of remembrance, though its style is commonplace.   In most of the other novels the subject is considered as just one of many city interests which claim the attention of the writer, and it suffers from the fact that it is forced, in competition with more alluring topics, to take a minor position.

CHAPTER VI

THE POLITICAL LIFE OF THE CITY

Political conditions in the three cities here studied have not received as great attention as have the social conditions, possibly because politics has generally been an unpopular field of endeavor for the man who makes his home in the city, particularly the man of education or the social leader. It should be noted that the term "political" may be used, as it is here, in a broad sense so as to include subjects so diverse as city elections; the careers of ward-leaders and city-wide bosses; resistance on the part of the people to governmental laws and regulations; reform movements; and the women's rights movement. The latter may be regarded as political since it describes the struggle of women to obtain the right to participate in the direction of city and national affairs.

A very early reference on the part of our novelists to political affairs in the city is the highly satirical one found in *Modern Chivalry* (1792). There Captain Farrago is shown arriving in the then American metropolis, Philadelphia, in time to witness an election. He is amazed to discover that all the candidates for office were "remarkably pot-bellied, and waddled in their gait." Upon inquiry, he learned that they were plentifully supplied with money, entertained extensively, sometimes fifty people at a time, and always ate and drank abundantly. This, combined with their inactive life, caused them to be so noticeably swollen. Brackenridge is here, of course, indulging in good-natured satire and is not to be taken any more seriously than he is in a previous episode in which he shows an election in an outlying district being won by a candidate with two kegs of whiskey and little else to recommend him over his opponent, a man of gravity and years of experience.

More serious but too vague to warrant consideration here are the huge political schemes of Ormond and Welbeck in the novels of Brockden Brown. Their plans are national and even world-wide in scope and have little connection with the political life of the city.

Passing into the nineteenth century and the third decade thereof, the searcher for political material in the city novel comes to a stop for a few moments at the year 1835 with *Clinton Bradshaw.* Another election draws his attention. The hero, not pot-bellied like Philadelphia's candidates in *Modern Chivalry,* but young and athletic, is shown in the midst of a bitter struggle with the father of the girl whom he hopes to marry. Both are candidates for representative in Congress from the same city district.   The press has waged a strong campaign against Bradshaw using all possible material it can discover, true or false regarding his earlier life. Finally, on the very day of the election, hand-bills are distributed accusing him of immorality. Bradshaw almost loses his sweetheart, as did Peter Sterling in a similar situation in Ford's celebrated novel of almost sixty years later, but since he is entirely innocent, it is fitting and proper that he should win the election and the girl also.

Thomas's handling of this and other political situations in the same novel is marked by a vividness and reality unusual for the time. The reader feels that the impressions of city and national politics there presented were the result of actual participation by the author—which may indeed be true, for as a young man in Baltimore in 1829, and several years later in Cincinnati, Thomas was well-known as a political orator.*

Abel Newt, in George W. Curtis' *Trumps,* is a direct antithesis of Clinton Bradshaw, for he is not in politics to reform city or national affairs but sofely for the graft that he can obtain. He and his city boss, General Belch and lesser satellites, have concocted a plan to get large sums of money from the passage of a land grant bill. Abel, despite the teaching of his father that no gentleman ever has anything to do with politics, accepts the nomination for Congress and is elected. At the capital he helps put the bill through. Thus, he is an early instance in the American novel of the young man of social importance entering city politics and yielding to its temptations to corruption of moral character. General Belch is frank to admit that he is in politics for his own individual profit. Later bosses in these novels were just

---

*See *Southern Literary Messenger,* iv, 297 (May, 1838).

as eager for graft but not as frank in their acknowledgment of that fact. Curtis's portrait of the city boss is a slight one and does not offer nearly as much information about the habits of such an individual as the later sketches by Fawcett and Ford.

Curtis and Thomas in the two novels just noted were writing about political life of the late twenties and early thirties. Almost three decades later city politics became nationalized with the outbreak of the Civil War. City elections and the corrupt methods of the city political boss give way temporarily to new topics. These include the slacker parading the streets wearing the national uniform though not properly enlisted in any branch of its defence; the dishonest recruiting officer who deceives the public as to the number of men he had enrolled in his regiment in order to obtain excessive amounts of food, clothing, and other supplies; the use of shoddy in making clothing for the army, insuring enormous profit for the manufacturers; the deception practiced by city merchants who, after promising to continue the pay of clerks absent in the Union army, promptly forgot their word after the men had once left the city. These may all be found in two novels of the early years of the war written in 1863 by Henry Morford: *The Days of Shoddy* and *Shoulder Straps*. They are valuable for their presentation of little-known details about the political conditions of New York in the days of the great struggle. One is surprised that the war plays such an insignificant part in the city's life. If one is to accept Morford's picture as a true one, it would seem that many able-bodied men in the city felt themselves under no obligation to join the army. Certain individuals were held up to ridicule as slackers, and one in particular, Colonel Bancker, was made to appear an utter coward for not attempting to stop a runaway carriage. It is significant, however, that the young hero, Frank Wallace, who fearlessly halted the frightened horses on that occasion and saved several lives, was himself never troubled about enlistment. And his patriotic sweetheart never mentioned his neglected duty, nor thought it incongruous that such a brave gallant should not be fighting at the front. One character, Haviland, finds after a three months' campaign that he had "enough of war." The author explains that he has not faltered in patriotism or purpose, but "the sweet blonde hair of his wife twines around him and the clinging pressure of her lips holds him fast."

The presence of "shoddying" of many varieties in New York and other Northern cities during the Civil War is now accepted as authentic, and there is no doubt of the prevalence of the military slacker. The indifference of whole groups of citizens to the conflict, which Morford depicts, is, on the other hand, surprising to the average reader, but is not at variance with historical accounts of the city's war-time life. Although New York was loyal to the Union and played a prominent part in its preservation, it is true that many of her citizens never took active part in the war. The same is true also of Philadelphia, as Morford showed in a third Civil War novel, *The Coward* (1864).

Morford's novels are not of high grade as literature, since they are filled with sentimentality and melodramatic situations. He had a journalist's ability for seeing the value of certain story incidents that he found in the city, but he was unable to develop them into novels with permanent qualities.

E. P. Roe's handling of the war scene in the same city shows the inhabitants in active revolt against the Government's military conscription plan. This is found in his *An Original Belle* (1885). Roe had served through the war as an army chaplain and was therefore writing of problems that he understood from personal experience. In some of his detailed accounts of campaigns of the war, he writes like an historian and not a novelist, but in dealing with the New York draft riots of July, 1863, he carries his leading characters into the very centre of the action, and creates a stirring series of incidents that hold the attention. Willard Merwyn, the hero, proves his loyalty to the Union cause and his courage as he joins with city police and state militia in fighting the mob in an effort to protect city property, enforce the law, and at the same time protect his sweetheart and her father.

Roe's treatment of the struggle between the forces of the law and the unruly, liquor-maddened mob is realistic. A contest for the possession of a factory containing carbines is described by him as a "life-and-death encounter between a handful of policemen and a grimy, desperate band of ruffians, cornered like rats, and resolved to sell their lives dearly." The insurrection lasted three days with various mobs "fighting, plundering, burning, . . . chasing and murdering negroes," simultaneously in widely-scattered sections of the city. At last, soldiers supplementing the efforts of the police and volunteers succeed in quelling the rioters by the use of howitzers and muskets. Many were killed or wounded, both men and women. Roe places the blame for the riots upon the administration for "ordering the draft to be inaugurated at a time when the city was stripped of its militia."

The Civil War is indirectly connected with *The House of a Merchant Prince* (1883), for the New York merchant Rodman Harvey made his fortune during and shortly after that war and his final discomfiture came as the result of his alleged treason in connection with it. In the early part of the novel the reader finds him still unsatisfied after amassing his millions. His ambition now turns towards political fame and at the opening of his palatial new home on Fifth Avenue he holds an elaborate reception for President Hayes. On later occasions he is host to other celebrities such as brother merchants, magnates of the stock exchange or of the railroads, military officers, high functionaries of state and scions of nobility. His ambitions are not directed towards amelioration of his own city's political world. That would presumably offer him too little glory and might involve him in bitter and distasteful struggles with the powerful Tammany organization. But he turns his eye towards Washington and a vacancy existing in the President's cabinet. At a civic meeting the merchant meets with a decisive blow to his political aspirations. As an important official of the Civic Reform Association, he is about to make a report in an open meeting, when certain enemies combine against him and publicly charge him with having committed treason against the United States at the outbreak of the war. Further, they accuse him of forgery at a critical period in his financial career. Although he knows that he is innocent of both charges, his over-wrought nerves cannot withstand the shock caused by the suddenness and severity of the attack against him. He suffers a paralytic stroke and remains an invalid for the rest of his life. His political ambitions are, of course, utterly squelched and justice is served, for punishment at last overtakes the war profiteer after he has enjoyed a long immunity.

Bishop's novel abounds in city atmosphere which is skilfully presented, but it is marred somewhat by absence of any dominating motive or outstanding character. The city merchant comes as close as any one towards filling this post. His political ambitions provide the author with some informative scenes illustrating the close relationship between social and political affairs in the city's life, but there are no important revelations of contemporary political conditions in New York. The merchant is carefully delineated but is not as real as some of the later political personages to be met with in novels by Mrs. Davis and P. L. Ford. Bishop makes him a type of unsatisfied ambition and seems to desire to moralize on the fact that he has a home which is one of the show places of the city but is not contented and will not take a needed rest from business toil. Inevitably then comes the physical break-down when he tries to add political success to the commercial success and the social esteem which his millions have won for him.

The enormous strength of city political rings in the seventies and their power to wreck human lives form the topics of several contemporary novels. The first, *Five Hundred Majority; or The Days of Tammany,* was written in 1872 by J. F. Hume under the pseudonym of Willys Niles. It relates the coming of a young farmer boy, Clinton Maintland, to New York city, with an ambition to learn law. For him that city is the centre of creation, but his sweetheart Margaret Kortright has the characteristic bucolic fear of it. Clinton wants to be a somebody and not just a clodhopper in a small town. He gets into New York politics, runs for legislature, as most of these young politicians seem to do, and defeats his opponent, Gordon Seacrist, by five hundred votes. But the latter is the son of the Tammany boss and uses the power of that organization to have Clinton imprisoned, and in the interval plots to win Margaret Kortright for himself. In such a situation the hero must be released from prison in order to rescue the heroine. As the story is mostly melodrama, the reader expects to find the villain and the unsuspecting heroine halted at the altar, and he is not disappointed. A former wife of young Seacrist makes a sudden and inconvenient appearance. Clinton recovers his sweetheart, determines wisely to abandon further pursuit of city politics and takes his bride back with him to Willowford, where fortunately she has "ample possessions." Henceforth, he has no desire to return to wicked New York, for he feels that he could not reconcile himself to living in a community governed by Tammany Hall. This novel seems amateurish and sentimental to the present-day reader, but it is significant as an attempt to expose the corruption of New York politics at a time when Tammany was at the height of its power.

The second of the novels dealing with city political rings is *John Andross,* written by Mrs. R. H. Davis in 1874. This is a much better novel and is notable for its fearless revelation of the operations of the Whiskey Ring in Philadelphia and its efforts to control legislation at the state capital at Harrisburg. The book contains a realistic account of the deep hold that the Ring has on John Andross, a young man weak-willed, but otherwise quite prepossessing. After escaping from its clutches for a time, he is re-captured and forced to re-enter its service and become the agent for bribing legislators.

In Houston Laird, the head of the Ring, Mrs. Davis portrayed a character who is entirely unscrupulous about attaining his purposes through bribery, or even by violence. He had the use of professional strong men who would commit murder at his behest, if necessary. His control over Andross was a cowardly one— the threat of the public disclosure of an act of dishonesty which his father had committed many years before his death.

In accordance with her usual practice, Mrs. Davis does not make Laird entirely unworthy of sympathy, though his evil qualities greatly exceed his good ones. In his ostentatious charitable work, he plays the hypocrite, for superintendence of city Christian associations, aged workmen's homes, and hospitals can hardly be reconciled with his crimes committed under the guise of politics. The author carefully explains, however, that there was in his nature a trait or sixth sense that prevented him from ever saying a coarse word before his children or men whom he respected for integrity. In his recreations, too, he showed good discrimination, for he did not gamble at the horse races but preferred a quiet day of fishing. At the theatre he did not relish the plays which had even a suggestion of the indecent. To quote the author's own words: " . . . When his friends filled their boxes at the Academy of Music, chuckling over the broad shoulders and broader jokes of the Opera Bouffe, . . . Laird jeered at them."* His taste was more sentimental, for "he went night after night to watch old Rip's parting with his daughter, and was not ashamed to be seen wiping the tears off as he came away." . . . He felt himself a better man after "listening to Joe Jefferson's wonderful rendition of nature or one of Thomas's noble symphonies."*

Houston Laird is one of the best portraits of the political boss that we shall find in this study. Mrs. Davis endowed him with human characteristics. She did not, as often happened in political fiction, make him a combination of all the evil traits that could be found flourishing in the political machine which he headed. Other persons in this novel who are well depicted are Andross and his friend Braddock; the flirtatious Anna Maddox; and Colonel Latimer, the Civil War veteran of honest and unsuspecting character who becomes the innocent tool of the Ring when he accepts Laird's appointment as Collector of Revenue in Philadelphia. The scenes in the latter city are vivid revelations of social and political conditions of the time. To some city dwellers honesty and poverty then seemed almost synonymous. Thus Braddock discovers that it is difficult to make a bare living in the Quaker City, and that it is worse in Washington. Companions whom he meets on city streets tell him:

> "There's no room for patient, honest effort in a city. You must have capital, or influence, or cheek, which is better than either. Money-making is a great game of grab, and a modest man stands no chance. Look at Fish, or Tweed, in New York. . . . Did they achieve success by modest industry?"†

Braddock perseveres with his modesty and his integrity, keeps away from the influence of the corrupt political machine and escapes the demoralization that comes to the character of his friend Andross. But his character is colorless, and the author succeeds in keeping the reader's sympathy fastened upon the

---

*Davis, Mrs. Rebecca Harding—"John Andross", New York, 1874, 83-84.
†ibid., 166.

more attractive Andross. In so doing she makes more tragic his ultimate fate. The hold of the Whiskey Ring had been broken when he made his sensational resignation from the state legislature, but his will had been hopelessly weakened by his long subservience to it.

Mrs. Davis was courageous in writing of whiskey rings in 1874, for they were then still active. In this same year Secretary of the Treasury Richardson uncovered a ring in St. Louis, which, with the aid of the supervisor of internal revenue there, had been defrauding the government annually of a million dollars in whiskey taxes.*

Machine politics again plays an important part in a city young man's public career in Robert Grant's *An Average Man* (1884). Woodberry Stoughton, friend of the spiritually minded Arthur Remington, who was mentioned in the chapter on religious life, is quite a different person from him in every way. As an example of the young man of good social connections entering into city governmental affairs, he reminds the reader of Abel Newt, the dissipated political adventurer of *Trumps,* but Stoughton is a reformer, an attitude of mind to which Newt never made any pretence. When he finds it difficult to make headway against the ward organization, Stoughton compromises with the opposition, discards his reform principles and immediately forges ahead. The meeting at which he is chosen to be the ward's Republican candidate is important for the picture there presented of typical city politicians of the time—the early eighties. One listens there to the spread-eagle oratory of the Honorable Mr. Dunn, a nominee for Congressman; and one meets Ramsay Whiting, leading member of the Civil Service Reform Club; and Hon. Cornelius French, a self-made man, that is, as Grant facetiously explains, a man "always looking out for himself before everything and everybody else, even including the party to which he belonged."† In his city position he came intimately "into contact—or rather into contract—with the civic needs, in the line of lamps, sewers, and pavements."†

---

*Bassett, John S.—"A Short History of the United States", New York, 1925, 651.
†Grant, Robert—"An Average Man", Boston, 1884, 149.

Stoughton serves two years in the legislature and then enters into a strenuous campaign for Congress. He has made money through his stock speculations—over $200,000 in all; and has married, but soon becomes tired of his wife and more interested in a woman who seems more intellectual. In the campaign for election, he again compromises with his principles, because he finds it absolutely essential, as he thinks, to spend money to insure his election. On one occasion he had refused a delegation that had solicited funds from him. This was a group of seven mechanics representing the Independent Ballot Boys. But when such a high dignitary in the city political affairs as the Hon. Alderman Dunn demands $30,000 from him to be given to the voters, the young candidate cannot refuse without seriously endangering his chances. Therefore he writes him a check for that amount, all of which, as events prove, is absolutely wasted, for he loses out on Election Day and finds himself almost destitute of money and threatened with a divorce suit from his wife.

The political scenes in *An Average Man* are subordinated to the scenes dealing with the city fortunes of the other young man of the story, Remington, but episodic as they are, they illustrate several common conditions, namely: (1) the tendency of reformers in city politics to succumb to the alluring attractions set before them by the well-organized city machine, fearing apparently that they cannot accomplish anything of importance without its assistance; and (2) the necessity of using money freely to obtain political office. The other side of the picture had not as yet been shown, that is, the efforts of a really honest and capable city reformer who cannot be side-tracked from his course by the strongest pressure of the political machine. Grant is not as successful in presenting the political life of the city as he was in the social life as found in *Unleavened Bread*, but the comparison is perhaps not a fair one since the later novel is greatly superior to *An Average Man*.

Participation in political affairs of a man with entrée into the highest social circles is found again in John Harrington, the chief character of F. Marion Crawford's *An American Politician* (1884). He is described as a great contrast to the usual run of Bostonians on account of his absorption in politics and good government. His speeches, though to the reader they seem monotonous and wearisome, are said to have had a great influence on his fellow-citizens. Crawford writes of him: "He said that things were wrong and should be put right; and when he said so for half an hour to a couple of thousand people, most of them were ready to follow him out of the hall and go and put them right on the spot, with their own hands."* But those who disapproved of Harrington warned their friends that some day he "would be seen heading a desperate mob of socialists in an assault upon the State House."* Despite these statements the reader does not find Harrington playing any significant role in the city government but exerting all his energies in national affairs. The picture of national problems is obscured by the inclusion of three mysterious men named alphabetically X, Y, and Z, who, though residing in London are able to wield a powerful influence in this country. They appreciate the worth of Harrington, so that when Mr. Z dies, the Bostonian is called to London to take his place. The appointment comes opportunely, for Harrington has just been refused a Senatorial post by the Massachusetts legislature, his rejection being caused principally by his unwillingness to bow the knee to Boston's political chief, one Patrick Ballymolloy. The appearance of the latter brings welcome relief to a story which is unusually dull for one written by Marion Crawford. Humor is abundant in the detailed description of Ballymolloy. He was said to be corpulent. No doubt he was a good trencherman like Houston Laird in Mrs. Davis's novel. He was truculent, with huge hands and feet and dirty finger nails ("of a hue which is made artificially fashionable in eastern countries, but which excites prejudice in western civilization from an undue display of real estate").† His mouth was "an immense cavity" and as to his nose, "it was one of the most surprising feats of nature's alchemy that a liquid so brown as that contained in the decanters on Patrick's sideboard should be able to produce and maintain anything so supernaturally red as Patrick's nose."† He wore a suit of "shiny black broadcloth and the front of his coat was irregularly but richly adorned with a profusion of grease spots of

---

*Crawford, F. Marion—"An American Politician", New York, 1884, 23.
†ibid., 220.

all sizes."* And 'from his heavy gold watch-chain depended a malachite seal of unusual greenness and brilliancy."* The only ornament missing to this typical city politician seems to be the inevitable diamond stick-pin.

The only other political reference in the novel worthy of notice is one which relates the tax-dodging habit of rich Bostonians by which they spend six months and a day in their country places, thus shifting a large percentage of their tax burdens to more economical regions. Crawford sarcastically comments: "It is a very equitable arrangement, for it is only the rich man who can save money in this way, while his poorer neighbor, who has no country seat to which he may escape, must pay to the uttermost farthing.   The system stimulates the impecunious to become wealthy and helps the rich to become richer.   It is, therefore, perfectly good and just."†

Boston life forms the subject of one of Henry James's few novels dealing with American city life—*The Bostonians* (1886). In this one may find a careful reproduction of the agitation of a group of Boston women of the 1870's for emancipation from what seemed to them man's tyranny over them.   Women had already made a successful inroad into business and professional life ; now they were striving for the ballot.   James shows his enthusiastic feminists meeting together at afternoon social functions and in public meetings, laboring to secure wider recognition for the cause.   The scenes are mostly in Boston, but on one occasion the reader is brought to New York to which the fame of Verena Tarrant as a psychic speaker has spread.   Verena speaks not her own message but just what she has been taught to say by her instructor and self-appointed director, Olive Chancellor. The latter is a strong-minded, intelligent woman—pale, nervous and intense—who makes life an extremely hard task for herself and is never so happy as when struggling and even suffering for political privileges for her sex.   After securing control of Verena from her father, Miss Chancellor prepared a long tour for her, beginning at Music Hall, Boston.   The description of this initial meeting provides the best scene in the novel and is one of the best

---

*ibid., 221.
†ibid., 281-2.

presentations in our literature of a city public gathering ending in confusion, as they often do when the guest of honor fails to appear, or is taken sick. In this case, Verena is prevented from speaking through the interference of her lover, Basil Ransom, who fears that her life may be ruined by continued contact with Miss Chancellor and therefore persuades her to leave the hall and go with him to New York, where they plan to be married. With his usual skill in presenting minute details, James misses none of the dramatic values of such a situation. He gives a vivid impression of the immense throng gathered to hear Verena, attracted there not so much by an interest in women's rights as by rumors of the mysterious power of the speaker. When she fails to appear on the platform long after the set hour, the crowd expresses its impatience by loud stamping of feet and clamoring. Her father tries to quiet them by telling them that she will positively appear in three minutes. In the ante-room where Verena is waiting, a contest takes place between Basil and Miss Chancellor for possession of the girl. Her agent, Mr. Filer, implores her to go out to the audience, reminding her that the city of Boston is there waiting for her. Outside, impatience at the delay continues, but after Verena leaves the auditorium and Miss Chancellor appears on the stage and explains the matter as best she can, the vast audience is somewhat pacified. James comments that the people were evidently not going to hurl the benches at Miss Chancellor, and one of the characters declares that "even when exasperated, a Boston audience is not ungenerous." But some of the distinguished guests are angry and they express bitter condemnation of that indefinite, inanimate object, "the management". The author's cleverness of phraseology is seen when he describes the face of one of them—a woman—as expressing "the well-bred surprise of a person who should have been asked out to dinner and seen the cloth pulled off the table."

Among the workers for women's freedom found in this novel, one of the most individual is Miss Birdseye, an old lady about eighty, who is said to be a survivor of Boston's abolitionist days and to have belonged at one time or other to "any and every league that had been founded for any purpose whatever, and was in love only with causes, and languished only for emancipations." Mrs.

Farrinder, a lecturer, works to "give the ballot to every woman in the country and to take the flowing bowl from every man."

The Bostonians may not be regarded as primarily a political novel since it stresses to such a large extent the social side of woman's life. But it can be said in praise of the author that he makes very interesting use of his political material and succeeds in bringing out those elements in it that would be most likely to appeal to his readers. At the same time he instructs them in regard to the progress of a vital movement of the city's history. Other city novels could be cited to show that their authors too were aware of the efforts being made to change the political status of women, but none gives so effective a treatment of the subject as this one.

No account of city politics during the nineteenth century would be complete without mention of the political drone who owes his position to his ability to bring in votes for his leaders, and who as a reward, receives a sinecure at City Hall or other public building. There he works with one eye constantly on the clock and the other on the calendar, as he mentally calculates the days that must elapse before the next pay envelope will be handed him. Henry Harland has caught the spirit of such life remarkably well in a few pages in his *Grandison Mather*. Tom Gardiner has secured an easy berth as clerk in the Prothonotary's office in New York city. His duties consist merely of keeping a record of documents, filing them, and producing them whenever they are called for. Several of his associates are typical office holders. One, Mr. Temple, very talkative, hates his position, though he has worked at it for a long time. He regards it as beneath his abilities and education. He is old, dresses in black broad-cloth and inserts French phrases frequently into his conversation. The head of the Accounting Department, Mr. Galligan, is a better example. Harland's portrait of him, slightly exaggerated as it is, is delightfully humorous. As a boss, he is privileged to sit unrebuked with feet on top of his desk and highly-polished stove-pipe hat shoved down over his forehead. A spittoon is conveniently situated on the floor beside him. In appearance he resembles "an ox crossed with a bull-dog." The diamond which was missed in Crawford's caricature of Ballymolloy is here conspicuous in Galligan's shirt front, but the author is not certain that it is a real one. The fact that he wears a paper collar seems an argument against the genuineness of the jewel. A gold watch-chain crosses his waistcoat. His trousers were reported to be of a decided check pattern and enclosed his huge legs like tights. "Altogether", the author states, "you would have known him instantly for one of three things—a burglar, a prize-fighter, or a New York politician."* As to occupation, "he was doing nothing but sitting at ease . . . with his feet atop his table, slowly ruminating upon his tooth-pick."*

Humor such as Harland introduced into the representation of a city's political boss was replaced by grim seriousness and profound disgust in the case of Edgar Fawcett's drawing of Boss Tweed in *A New York Family* (1891). Tweed was, of course, a real person, and the most notoriously dishonest political leader in the history of American cities. To insert an historical figure in a novel is not an easy task, and it is made much more difficult if, as in Fawcett's novel, the individual was one as well remembered by older New York citizens as Tweed, who had been dead for only thirteen years when the novel was published. His portrait is not a notable one, nor are the few scenes in which he appears, at all well done. Indeed, the illustrations or caricatures by Thomas Nast convey almost as real an impression of Tweed as do Fawcett's word pictures. The facts presented about his character and his habits are of value only as they add to or compare with the portraits already presented of city bosses.

The author's discussion of political life in New York of the seventies is punctuated with severe criticism of his townsmen's apathy to the serious effects of the audacities committed by Tweed and his confederates. He writes that "a torpor had fallen upon the vast town, and it let itself be robbed with ruthless greed. . . . And yet the city, with its thousands of decent dwellers, had no doubt that thieves ruled it. Helpless it surely was not; in failing to rise and help itself the languor it showed was almost unparalleled by any human precedent."†

---

*Harland, Henry—"Grandison Mather", New York, 1889, 238-9.
†Fawcett, Edgar—"A New York Family", New York, 1891, 109.

As to Tweed's personal appearance, Fawcett notes "his middle-aged corpulency still hinting of the fire-boy, rough, and loafer he had been, with his palish, long-nosed, and narrow-eyed visage telling of the animalisms that stained his private life, and with his pell-mell and spluttering speech a massacre of syntax when it was not also a riot of oaths."*

The secret of his towering dominance over his fellow-citizens is declared to lie in his "nerves of iron, titanic audacity" and piercing, lucid brain.   Fawcett states that he had no cultivation, no accomplishments, hardly what might be called a common education, but by his ingenuity in gaining control over the establishments and agencies that supplied the city's needs, this "Napoleon of swindlers" was able to amass twenty million dollars.

The scene in which two fledgling lawyers endeavor to out-blackmail Tweed, the mighty master of blackmail, is evidently introduced, as are all the Tweed episodes, in order to allow the author to preach against the city's supposed return in his own day to its former corruption. He inquires, "Has the languor of voters abated in any marked way? Do pure men seek candidacies oftener than of old? and when they do, and win at elections, are they apt to breast currents of evil or let themselves drift with its venal tides?"†   The answers, if given by the author, would not be favorable to the citizens, as may be judged by this further statement: "The metropolis may not be cursed at this hour by so gigantic a pest as Tweed, but who shall dare to state that those trusted with the enactment of city laws are not often made in his fell though feebler likeness?   It is a frightful thought that the corroding vitriol of reformation should not have dissipated these low larcenies and made their recurrence impossible."‡

The reader must feel that, on the whole, Fawcett's treatment of Tweed is very little improvement on the historical accounts of his career, which makes no pretence to literary quality.   To the person reading for the first time about Tammany's corruption under Tweedism, the novel will bring adequate information, but it will not give him the stimulus that he should expect to obtain from perusal of a work of literature.   The portrait of Tweed

*ibid., 110.
†ibid., 186-7.

himself is the conventional one found in most works of fiction dealing with political bosses. It compares unfavorably with the portrait which Mrs. Davis makes of Houston Laird. The other political characters, too, in Fawcett's work—those who suffer from Tweed's methods—are not as subtly drawn as those found in *John Andross*.

The city boss of Paul Leicester Ford's *The Honorable Peter Sterling* (1894) is an infinitely higher type of individual than those already noted in this review: Laird, Ballymolloy, or Tweed. Fawcett's criticism of the absence of able men in politics receives an adequate reply in Sterling in this novel. Whether he is an idealized portrait of the real flesh-and-blood "boss" is a question difficult to answer. Professor Allan Nevins has asserted that the novel was based partly on actual experiences of the author during an unsuccessful attempt to enter politics in the first ward in Brooklyn.* It was raised to a best-seller by the popular impression that its hero was modelled upon Grover Cleveland. This Ford denied, saying that Sterling was suggested not by one but by several public men. The facts are undeniable that he was intended for an educated man of good family, and one not in entire sympathy with the activities or inactivities of that group of persons designated familiarly as Society.

Sterling's entrance upon a political career was not a sacrifice to personal ambition or even to pride of family. It was simply the most obvious thing for him to do. As a young lawyer without practice, and without influence, and a stranger in a large city, he naturally seized upon the first opportunity that offered itself. That was in the life of his young friends, the tenement-house children of the Sixth Ward. Intimate association with them, acting as their big brother, had proved to be for him much more pleasant and profitable than companionship with the uninspiring clerks of the Bleecker Street boarding-house where he had lodged during his earliest days in the city. When one of these protégées of his became ill and died as a result of drinking impure milk, Sterling immediately began an exhaustive investigation that finally took him to the Governor's office at Albany. Appointed special

---

*See article on Paul Leicester Ford by Allan Nevins in the Dictionary of American Biography, 1931, vol. 6, 517.

counsel for the State, he sued the offending Milking Company
and in his prosecution showed his earnest solicitude for the welfare of the common people by his emphatic declaration that this
"is the case of the tenement-house children against the inhumanity
of man's greed." City-wide recognition of his powers as a lawyer
followed, but Sterling remained true to his Sixth Ward and the
men and women there who revered him as one of their own kind
for his mercy to their children and for his refusal to hold himself
superior to them on account of his broader education and cleaner
moral character. He had an opportunity to enter into New York
social circles, for Miss De Voe, equally famous for lineage, wealth
and philanthropy, had expressed her approval of his work and
had contributed $500 to help him carry on his tenement charities.
Sterling, however, preferred to devote his leisure hours to the
cultivation of the friendship of rough, but loyal characters like
saloon-keeper Dennis Moriarity and the men who frequented his
and other saloons. Therefore, it was proper that he should have
been selected to represent the Ward at the state assembly. His
fearlessness and honesty in dealing with the political affairs of
that district led eventually to his promotion to the political leadership of the whole city, an honor which he thoroughly deserved,
but one which a man of his high integrity rarely receives.

Peter Sterling's methods of holding his exalted position were
not different from those of most political leaders, for like all such
men, he carefully learned of the needs of his people and then took
active charge of the means used to supply those needs. His
theory was that ordinary men in want were too self-respecting to
go to the big charities or to rich men for aid but would come to
him, because they trusted him. Sterling was more sincere in
treatment of the poor than most bosses and was content to remain
disinterested and not try to use his great influence in gaining a
fortune by illegal manipulation of city contracts. He stands elevated too above the reformer who dabbles in the city's politics
at the same time that he has other occupations to which he devotes
a greater part of his time. By giving a large share of his energies
to city and state politics, Sterling was sacrificing his own private
benefit. This is perhaps the most significant fact to be learned
from the novel and is not brought out clearly until Sterling

receives the nomination for Governor. Then the reader is informed that the prospect for the new post was not entirely pleasing to him, for it entailed upon him the abandonment of $50,000 a year law practice which had taken him seventeen years to develop. And, what he could not foresee, the campaign was to entangle him in a charge of scandal that almost ruined him both politically and socially. One cannot but believe, however, that in the end he considered all these trials as no more than painful but necessary steps towards final victory. The author's teaching still should abide with the reader. This can be found best expressed in Sterling's own declaration that the really successful merchant, banker, or professional man cannot or will not take time to work in politics; and, therefore, the city has to be content with the efforts of second-rate men, or of reformers who quarrel among themselves, or of corrupt self-seekers who care nothing for the city's real betterment.

Ford's novel is the best illustration of the novel dealing with city political life that can be obtained from this whole period, that is, of course, among novels with scene laid in New York, Philadelphia, or Boston. Its characters are well drawn; its scenes are interesting; and its presentation of the facts about a politician's career is notable for clarity and completeness. The novel was important too because it showed the great amount of good which an honest, skilful, well-trained leader could accomplish by entering whole-heartedly into the city's political life.

A comprehensive gance at all the novels studied in this chapter will reveal the presence of some good-natured raillery and some serious criticism of city political methods. The city boss has been traced in the novel from the twenties and thirties to the end of the century, and our novelists have been shown intensely in earnest in exposing the great evils caused by these men through their political organizations. In every case but one they failed to consider the important part which an upright, courageous leader could play in remedying such evils. Until the coming of Ford's novel readers were apparently supposed to believe that the cities contained no honest bosses. His novel was consequently a great enlightenment and an incentive to decent men to emulate Sterling.

The old superstitution that gentlemen do not soil their hands by entering into the vulgar business of city politics is refuted in at least four instances in these novels. Two of them are young men who, though coming from good families and well fortified with education, ruin their own lives in politics and hence are arguments against the breaking down of the old superstition. On the other hand, arguments for the participation of high-class men in city politics are found in Harrington who exerts a perceptible influence for good upon his fellow-Bostonians and is said to encourage them into reform activities; and, best of all, in Peter Sterling, with his combination of good breeding and good education, and training in the fundamentals of politics. He is the supreme example of one qualified in all essentials to lead American cities out of the mire and stench of political corruption.

Like those novelists who dealt with the religious, and the literary-artistic phases of the life of the city, those treating of its political life did not often devote the major portion of their efforts to that particular topic. In general, their method was to include political material in their novels in the form of separate episodes in the careers of their principal characters. Five novels, however, were mainly concerned with political matters: *Five Hundred Majority,* a book of minor importance; *John Andross,* an intensive study of a young man whose life-career is ruined by the Whiskey Ring; *An American Politician,* which adds little to our knowledge of city politics, being mostly national in its interest; *The Bostonians,* an elaborate and entertaining study of the women's rights movement as it affected Boston social circles; and, finally, *The Honorable Peter Sterling,* the most sustained and most significant presentation of municipal political problems to be found among the city novels coming under this study.

CHAPTER VII

Conclusions

The student of city life, as contemporaneously interpreted by the novel, early becomes impressed with the fact that in order to obtain a complete picture of that life he must at times beat the dust from aged-worn volumes that have lain for years in peaceful obscurity. Some of these forgotten novels may yield only one or two city incidents, but if they have anything at all to add to the whole picture, they are worth careful consideration.

It has been frequently observed in the course of this work that our novelists rarely confined their attention to any one phase of city life. In some cases it would seem that they have tried to touch upon all its phases, and to accomplish this have used a series of short episodes. These, isolated though they are, have a value, for when they supplement the impression produced by a more sustained, unified narrative, they help to produce a fairly comprehensive, though not quite complete history of the city.

It is surprising to find so many important events, habits, and customs of urban life recorded within these novels. A list of the most noteworthy of these should include the following: the yellow-fever epidemics of Philadelphia and New York in the late eighteenth and early nineteenth centuries; the prevalence of duelling in settling disputes of honor; the frequency of religious revivals from 1830 to 1870; the practice of using shoddy in army clothing during the Civil War, especially in New York city; the constant migration of men, young and old, to the cities to seek their fortunes, a movement particularly noticeable in the decades after the Civil War; the appearance in the city about the same time of the millionaire and his tendency to suffer from physical collapse through over-work; the attempts of new religious beliefs like Spiritualism and the various forms of faith-healing to obtain a foothold in the large cities; the growth of city political "rings" led by corrupt bosses; and, in the last years of the century the development of the institutional church with its city-wide relief program. Some of these topics later received glamorous attention from our historical novelists, whose adaptations of them offer instructive comparisons with realistic treatments of the same topics by contemporary novelists.

The two greatest attractions in city life for our novelists were found in the struggle for success and in the social scene. Traces of the first of these themes may be found in almost all the novels. It inspired some of the best novels of the whole group. Writers like Brown, Taylor, Howells, Harland, Warner, Ford, Matthews and Grant were greatly interested in the individual's efforts to achieve distinction in the city as man of letters, artist, musician, doctor, or business man. Outstanding illustrations of this success-or-failure motive were collected into one chapter, but other instances can readily be traced in the other chapters, as, for example, *The Honorable Peter Sterling,* which presents a struggle for success in the political life of the city. The universality of the appeal of this theme is explained by the fact that it represents the struggle for existence in which all human beings take part. Closely allied to it is the social theme, which represents man's efforts to distinguish himself in relationships with his fellow-citizens. Most of the novelists of the city touched upon this theme. Some of them centered their attention upon the newly rich; some were attracted by the well-established families; others, aroused by the apparent inequalities of social opportunities in city life, became bitter in criticism of the life of the social leaders, and wrote sensational exposures of their alleged faults. The conservative attitude in regard to the whole problem was presented by Mrs. Mowatt, Mrs. Kirk, Howells, Crawford, Warner, and Grant.

Most of the contributors to fiction of the city were delighted in writing about it, but their anxiety to reveal its complex nature led them at times to include too many of its features in one novel. Also, in their enthusiasm they were carried occasionally into too lengthy descriptions of some of its external aspects. Unity is often seriously lacking in their novels—a condition which is not surprising when one realizes how multiform the city itself is. But the ability to centre the attention upon a single segment of the city's diverse life is the secret of success with the city novel, and those few writers who could do this well created the best novels. Howells had this ability, and it is significant that his work stands pre-eminent in three sections of this study, namely, the chapters dealing with the struggle for success in the city, its religious life, and its social life. For the purpose of learning the customs of people of the city in his time, and for faithful, interesting presentation of their problems, Howells' novels are invaluable. His emphasis was always upon the common, everyday features of city life, but it is with them that the interest of the social historian of the city chiefly lies. Other novelists also, though to a less degree, succeeded in writing novels of the city that contain an unified effect. Among these may be named Taylor, Winthrop, James, Mrs. Kirk, Bunner, Harland, Crane, Glasgow, and Grant.

Many novelists who wrote about the city exhibited literary traits which made their works important for their own age but did not in every case earn them permanent recognition. Among earlier writers Charles Brockden Brown is significant because he painted vivid scenes of plague-beset cities; Frederick W. Thomas is noteworthy because of his anxiety to reproduce actual living conditions as he found them in our large centres, thus providing present-day readers with a valuable check upon the exaggerated pictures of the city painted by his contemporary Theodore Fay. Miss Sedgwick was also interested in painting faithful pictures of the cities and their people and in addition stressed the moral aspects of the city's life.

In the sixties and seventies the reproduction of realistic phases of life in American cities was continued in entertaining novels written by Bayard Taylor, George W. Curtis, Theodore Winthrop, and Rebecca Harding Davis. As already noted, the eighties and nineties saw the greatest outpouring of novels of urban life. Generally speaking, those years brought the most notable literary productions. Howells no doubt created the greatest number of them. Edgar Fawcett was more prolific but not nearly so great an artist from the standpoint of style, accuracy of painting the city's life, or ability in drawing character. Brander Matthews was reminiscent of Howells in his local color studies of New York city in his short stories and novels but his talents were not so eminent as those of Howells.

Idealism and dignity of style are marked characteristics of the novels of Henry C. Bunner and Henry Harland who wrote in the same period. Both specialized in the colorful life of New York's foreign colonies and vividly pictured the courageous struggle of their inhabitants for success in artistic or literary circles.

Vastly different was the emphasis found in the urban novels of F. Marion Crawford, Charles Dudley Warner, and Arlo Bates who wrote attractive studies of the social careers of native Americans of the well-to-do classes. Crawford's novels of the American city, while not so important as his novels with a foreign setting, are superior to a great number of urban novels written at the same time. Similar praise may be accorded Warner's trilogy of New York novels. In Arlo Bates one finds satire and epigram very much in the style of Henry James.

Robert Grant and Mrs. Ellen Olney Kirk also showed a keen interest in the social life of the city. Their works ranked high among novels of their time. Indeed Grant's *Unleavened Bread* is a memorable novel and one which is still valuable for its penetrating insight into social relationships.

In searching for local-color touches of urban life, one should not rely entirely upon the novel but should consult also the short story. The latter is as valuable as the novel and sometimes better illustrations of certain phases of urban life may be obtained from it than from the longer narrative. It should be remembered that some of the writers of fiction here considered had talents which were more readily adapted to the short story than to the novel. An instance in question is Brander Matthews. Others, not treated here at all, wrote illuminating fiction on the city, using exclusively the form of the short story. They must not be neglected if one is to obtain the complete fictional picture of the city.

When one compares the number of novels dealing with the life of the city that show excellence of literary quality with the total number of novels upon that subject, one notes at once that the ratio of excellence is a small one. Comfort may, however, be obtained from the fact that what some novels lacked in artistic achievement they made up in earnestness of intention. There are very few which do not have a semblance of merit and of value for the earnest reader, and by using all of the novels, one may obtain a veritable cyclopedia of facts about life in American cities from 1789 to 1900.

BIBLIOGRAPHY

The following is a list of books and articles found helpful in studying life in New York, Philadelphia, and Boston, 1789-1900, and in searching for and studying contemporary novels describing that life.

Bacon, Corinne—compiler of Standard Catalogue. Fiction Section. New York. H. W. Wilson Co. 1931.

Baker, Ernest A.—A Descriptive Guide to the Best Fiction in English. New York, 1914.

Bassett, John S.—A Short History of the United States. N. Y., 1925.

Beard, Charles A. and *Mary R.*—The Rise of American Civilization. 2 v. N. Y., 1927.

Boston Public Library Catalogue of English Prose Fiction. August, 1885, supplement, 1897.

Brown, Henry Collins—editor, Valentine's Manual of Old New York, 1926.

Cambridge History of American Literature. 4 v. N. Y., 1917-1921, especially bibliographies to chapters vi and vii in Book II and chapter xi in Book III, dealing particularly with prose fiction.

Dixson, Zella Allen—The Comprehensive Subject Index to Universal Prose Fiction. N. Y., 1897.

Faulkner, Harold U.—The Quest for Social Justice. 1898-1914, N. Y., 1931.

Fish, Carl R.—The Rise of the Common Man. N. Y., 1927.

Foley, P. K.—American Authors, 1795-1895. A Bibliography. Boston, 1897.

Garrison, Winfred E.—The March of Faith: The Story of Religion in America Since 1865. N. Y., 1933.

Griswold, Rufus Wilmot—The Prose Writers of America—Phila., 1847.

Griswold, W. M.—A Descriptive List of Novels and Tales Dealing with American City Life. Cambridge, 1891.

Hone, Philip—Diary. Edited by Allan Nevins. New York, 1927. 2 v.

Jackson, Joseph—Bibliography of the works of George Lippard in Penna. Magazine of History and Biography, LIV. April, 1930, 131-154.

Jackson, Joseph—Encyclopedia of Philadelphia. Harrisburg, 1931-33. 4 v.

Johnson, Allen and Dumas Malone, editors of Dictionary of American Biography. (20 v., N. Y., 1928, in progress).

Loshe, Lillie D.—The Early American Novel. Columbia Univ., 1907, reprinted, 1930.

McMaster, John B.—A History of the People of the United States from the Revolution to the Civil War. 8v., 1913.

Maurice, Arthur Bartlett—New York in Fiction. N. Y., 1901.

Morse, J. H.—Native Element in American Fiction before the War. Century Magazine, 4: 288; 362.

Moss, Frank—The American Metropolis from Knickerbocker Days to the Present Time. New York City Life in All Its Various Phases. 3 v. New York, 1897.

Nevins, Allan—American Social History as Recorded by British Travellers. N. Y., 1923.

Nevins, Allan—The Emergence of Modern America, 1865-1878. N. Y., 1927.

Oberholtzer, Ellis P.—A Literary History of Philadelphia. Phila., 1906.

Oberholtzer, Ellis P.—History of the United States since the Civil War. New York, 1917. 4 v.

Pattee, Fred L.—A History of American Literature since 1870. N. Y., 1915.

Pattee, Fred L.—The Development of the American Short Story, N. Y., 1923.

Pearson, Edmund—Queer Books. N. Y., 1928.

Scharf, J. Thomas and Thompson Westcott—History of Philadelphia, 1609-1884. 3 v., Phila., 1884.

Schlesinger, Arthur M.—The Rise of the City, 1878-1898. N. Y., 1933.

Shackleton, Robert—The Book of Boston. Phila., 1917.

Smith, Theodore C.—Parties and Slavery, 1850-1859. 1906. v. 18 of American Nation: a History.

Strong, Josiah—Religious Movements for Social Betterment. N. Y., 1900.

Sweet, W. W.—The Story of Religions in America. N. Y., 1930.

Van Doren, Carl—The American Novel. N. Y., 1921.

Weber, A. F.—The Growth of Cities in the Nineteenth Century. Columbia Univ. Studies. XI, 1899.

Wegelin, Oscar—Early American Fiction, 1774-1830. Rev. ed., N. Y., 1913.

Werner, M. R.—Tammany Hall. N. Y., 1928.

Wilson, James G.—The Memorial History of the City of New York from its first settlement to the year 1892. N. Y., 1892. 4 v.

Wilson, Rufus R.—New York: Old and New. Its Story, Streets, and Landmarks. Phila., 1902.

Winson, J.—Editor, Memorial History of Boston, 1630-1880. Boston, 1880-1881. 4 v.

Young, John R.—Editor, Memorial History of the City of Philadelphia from its First Settlement to the Year 1895. 2 v.

AMERICAN NOVELS DEALING WITH CITY LIFE

The following is a list of American novels which illustrate contemporary life in the cities of New York, Philadelphia, and Boston during the period 1789-1900. Only those books have been included which I have been able to examine personally. The arrangement is alphabetical by authors. After the title, follow in order the place of publication, name of the publishers, and the date. If no place of publication is inserted, New York is to be understood. The date is, in most cases, that of the first publication in book form.

ANONYMOUS

The Power of Sympathy. 1789. Reprinted, Boston, Cupples and Patterson, 1894.

The Hapless Orphan. By an American Lady, Boston, 2 v., 1793.

Monima; or, The Beggar Girl. Written by a Lady of Philadelphia. Phila., 1803.

Laura. By a Lady of Philadelphia. Phila., Bradford and Inskeep, 1809.

ARTHUR, TIMOTHY S.

Three Years in a Man-Trap. Phila., J. M. Stoddart, 1872.

Cast Adrift. Phila., J. M. Stoddart, 1873.

BATES, ARLO

The Pagans. H. Holt, 1884.

The Philistines. Boston, Ticknor, 1888.

The Puritans. Boston and New York, Houghton, 1898.

BENEDICT, F. L.

My Daughter Elinor. Harper, 1869.

BIRD, ROBERT MONTGOMERY

Sheppard Lee. 2 v. Harper, 1836.

Adventures of Robin Day. 2 v. Phila., Lea and Blanchard, 1839.

BISHOP, WILLIAM HENRY

The House of a Merchant Prince. Boston, Houghton, 1883.

BRACKENRIDGE, HUGH H.

Modern Chivalry. 2 v. Phila., 1792.

BROWN, CHARLES BROCKDEN

Ormond; or, The Secret Witness. 1799.

Arthur Mervyn; or, Memoirs of the year 1793. 2 v. Phila. and New York, 1799-1800.

BRUSH, MRS CHRISTINE (CHAPLIN)

The Colonel's Opera Cloak. Boston, Roberts Bros., 1888. First edition, 1879.

BUNNER, HENRY C.

The Midge. Scribner, 1886.

The Story of a New York House. Scribner, 1887.

BURDETT, CHARLES

Three Per Cent a Month; or, The Perils of Fast Living. Derby and Jackson, 1856.

The Second Marriage; or, A Daughter's Trials. Scribner, 1856.
Blonde and Brunette; or, The Gothamite Arcady: Appleton, 1858.
Chances and Changes. Appleton, 1869.

BUTTERWORTH, HEZEKIAH
Up from the Cape. Boston, Estes and Lauriat, 1883.

BYNNER, EDWIN LASSETER
Tritons. Boston, Lockwood, Brooks, 1878.

CABOT, ARTHUR W. and COGHILL, HOWARD
Two Gentlemen of Gotham. Cassell, 1887.

CARRUTHERS, WILLIAM A.
The Kentuckian in New York; or, The Adventures of Three Southerns. By a Virginian. 2 v. Harper, 1834.

CHAMBERS, JULIUS
On a Margin. Fords, Howard and Hulbert, 1884.

CLEMENS, SAMUEL L. and WARNER, CHARLES D.
The Gilded Age. 2 v. Harper, 1873.

COOPER, J. FENIMORE
Notions of the Americans. 2 v. Phila., Carey, Lea and Carey, 1828.
Home as Found. 2 v. Phila., Lea and Blanchard, 1838.
Le Mouchoir. An autobiographical romance. Wilson, 1843. Originally appeared in Graham's Magazine, Jan., 1843, to April, 1843. Reprinted as *Autobiography of a Pocket-Handkerchief.* Evanston, Ill., Golden-Booke Press, 1897.

CRANE, STEPHEN
Maggie, a Girl of the Streets. Appleton, 1896.
George's Mother. New York and London, Edward Arnold, 1896.
The Third Violet. Appleton, 1897.
Active Service. F. A. Stokes, 1899.

CRAWFORD, F. MARION
Dr. Claudius. Macmillan, 1883.
An American Politician. Macmillan, 1884.
The Three Fates. Macmillan, 1892.
Katharine Lauderdale. Macmillan, 1894.
The Ralstons. Macmillan, 1895.

CRUGER, MRS VAN RENSSELAER (Julien Gordon, pseud)
Poppaea. Phila., Lippincott, 1895.

CUMMINS, MARIA S.
The Lamplighter. Boston, J. P. Jewett, 1854.
Mabel Vaughan. Boston, Jewett, 1857.

CURTIS, GEORGE W.
Trumps. Harper, 1861. (*Harper's Weekly,* April 9, 1859, to Jan. 21, 1860).

DAVIS, MRS. REBECCA HARDING
Earthen Pitchers. Scribner's Monthly, Nov., 1873, to April, 1874.
John Andross. Orange Judd, 1874.
A Law Unto Herself. Phila., Lippincott, 1878.

DRAKE, JEANIE
The Metropolitans. Century, 1896.

EGGLESTON, EDWARD
The Faith Doctor. Appleton, 1891. (Century Magazine, Feb., 1891, to Oct., 1891).

ELLIOTT, SARAH B.
John Paget. H. Holt, 1893.

FAWCETT, EDGAR
A Hopeless Case. Boston, Houghton, 1880.
A Gentleman of Leisure. Boston, Houghton, 1881.
An Ambitious Woman. Boston, Houghton, 1884.
The Adventures of a Widow. Boston, Osgood, 1884.
Tinkling Cymbals. Boston, Osgood, 1884.
Rutherford. Funk and Wagnalls. 1884.
The House at High Bridge. Boston, Ticknor, 1887.
A Man's Will. Funk & Wagnalls, 1888.
Douglas Duane. Lippincott's Magazine, April, 1887.
Divided Lives. Chicago, Belford, Clarke, 1888.
Miriam Balestier. Chicago, Belford, Clarke, 1888.
Olivia Delaplaine. Boston, Ticknor, 1888.
A Demoralizing Marriage. Phila., Lippincott, 1889.
The Evil that Men Do. Belford, 1889.
A Daughter of Silence. Belford, 1890.
Fabian Dimitry. Chicago and New York, Rand, McNally, 1890.
How a Husband Forgave. Belford, 1890.
A New York Family. Cassell, 1891.
Women Must Weep. Chicago, Laird and Lee, 1891.
An Heir to Millions. Chicago, Schulte, 1892.
The Adopted Daughter. Chicago, Neeley, 1892.
American Push. Chicago, Schulte, 1892.
Her Fair Name. Merrill and Baker, 1894.
A Mild Barbarian. Appleton, 1894.
New York. Neeley, 1898.

FAY, THEODORE S.
Norman Leslie. A Tale of the Present Times. 2 v. Harper, 1835.
Sidney Clifton. 2 v. Harper, 1839.
Hoboken: a Romance of New York. 2 v. Harper, 1843.

FIELD, MRS. CAROLINE C.
Two Gentlemen of Boston. Boston, Ticknor, 1887.

FORD, MARY H.
Otto's Inspiration. Chicago, Griggs, 1895.

FORD, PAUL LEICESTER
The Honorable Peter Sterling. H. Holt, 1894.

FOSTER, GEORGE G
Celio; or, New York Above Ground and Under Ground. De Witt and Davenport, 1850.

GARLAND, HAMLIN
Jason Edwards. Appleton, 1897. First edition, Boston, Arena, 1892.

GAYLER, CHARLES
Out of the Streets. De Witt, 1869.

GLASGOW, ELLEN A. B.
The Descendant. New York and London, Harper, 1897.
Phases of an Inferior Planet. New York and London, Harper, 1898.

GRANT, ROBERT
The Confessions of a Frivolous Girl. Boston, Houghton, 1880.
An Average Man. Boston, Osgood, 1884.
The Carletons. Robert Bonner, 1891.
Mrs. Harold Stagg. Ledger Library, 1891.

A Romantic Young Lady. American Press Ass'n., 1891. First edition, Boston, 1886.
Reflections of a Married Man. Scribner, 1892.
Opinions of a Philosopher. Scribner, 1893.
Unleavened Bread. Scribner, 1900.

HARLAND, HENRY (Sidney Luska, pseud.)
As It Was Written. A Jewish Musician's Story. Cassell, 1885.
Mrs. Peixada. Cassel, 1886.
The Yoke of the Thorah. Cassell, 1887.
Grandison Mather. Cassell, 1889.

HARRISON, CONSTANCE CARY (Mrs. Burton Harrison)
The Story of Helen Troy. Harper, 1881.
The Anglomaniacs. Cassell, 1890.
Sweet Bells Out of Tune. Century, 1892.
A Bachelor Maid. Century, 1894.
Good Americans. Century, 1898.
A Circle of a Century. Century, 1899.

HAWTHORNE, JULIAN
Beatrix Randolph. Boston, Osgood, 1884.
Love—or a Name. Boston, Ticknor, 1885.
John Parmelee's Curse. Cassell, 1886.
An American Penman. Cassell, 1887.
The Great Bank Robbery. Cassell, 1887.
A Tragic Mystery. Cassell, 1887.
Section 558; or, The Fatal Letter. Cassell, 1888.
Another's Crime. Cassell, 1888.
A Dream and a Forgetting. Chicago, Belford, Clarke, 1888.

HOWELLS, WILLIAM DEAN
Their Wedding Journey. Boston, Houghton, 1872 (Atlantic Monthly, July, 1871, to Dec., 1871).
The Undiscovered Country. Boston and New York, Houghton, 1880.
A Modern Instance. Boston and New York, Houghton, 1882.
A Woman's Reason. Boston, Osgood, 1883.
The Rise of Silas Lapham. Boston and New York, Houghton, 1885.
The Minister's Charge. Boston, Ticknor, 1887. (Century Magazine, Feb., 1886, to Dec., 1886).
April Hopes. Harper, 1888.
A Hazard of New Fortunes. Harper, 1890.
The World of Chance. Harper, 1893.
The Coast of Bohemia. New York and London, Harper, 1893.
The Landlord at Lion's Head. Harper, 1897.

HUDSON, WILLIAM C. (Barclay North, pseud.)
The Diamond Button: Whose Was It? Cassell, 1889.
Jack Gordon, Knight-Errant, Gotham, 1883. Cassell, 1890.
Vivier of Vivier. Cassell, 1890.
On the Rack. Cassell, 1891.
The Man with a Thumb. Cassell, 1891.
Should She Have Left Him? Cassell, 1894.
An American Cavalier. Cassell, 1897.

HUME, J. F. (Willys Niles)
Five Hundred Majority; or, The Days of Tammany. Putnam, 1872.

INGRAHAM, JOSEPH H.
Edward Austin; or, The Hunting Flask. Boston, Gleason, 1842.
Frank Rivers; or, The Dangers of the Town. Boston, Williams, 1843.
The Miseries of New York. Boston, 1844.

Grace Weldon; or, Frederica, The Bonnet-Girl. New York and Boston, Williams, 1845.
Edward Manning. New York and Boston, Williams, 1847.
IRVING, JOHN T.
The Attorney; or, The Correspondence of John Quod. Samuel Hueston, 1853. (Knickerbocker Magazine, July, 1841, to Sept., 1842).
Harry Harson; or, The Benevolent Bachelor. Knickerbocker Magazine, March, 1843, to June, 1844. Published in book form, 1844(?).
The Old Doctor; or, Stray Leaves from My Journal. H. Long and Brother, no date.
JAMES, HENRY
Washington Square. Harper, 1881. (Harper's Monthly Magazine, July, 1880, to Dec., 1880).
The Bostonians. London and New York, Macmillan, 1886.
JOHNSON, EVELYN KIMBALL
An Errand Girl: a Romance of New York. Dillingham, 1889.
JUDD, SYLVESTER
Richard Edney and the Governor's Family. Boston, Phillips, Sampson, 1850.
KEENAN, HENRY F.
The Money-Makers. Appleton, 1885.
KIMBALL, RICHARD B.
Revelations of Wall Street. Knickerbocker Magazine, Jan., 1861, to May, 1862. Published as *Undercurrents of Wall Street.* Putnam, 1862.
Was IIe Successful? Carleton, 1864. Published as *His Idol,* Carleton, 1880.
Henry Powers (Banker). Carleton, 1868.
To-Day. Putnam's Magazine, 1869. Published as *To-Day, a Romance,* Carleton, 1870; and as *An Artful Widow,* Carleton, 1881.
KIRK, MRS. ELLEN OLNEY
Through Winding Ways. Phila., Lippincott, 1879.
Lesson in Love. Boston, Osgood, 1881.
Fairy Gold. Phila., Lippincott, 1883.
The Story of Margaret Kent. Boston, Ticknor, 1886.
Queen Money. Boston and New York, Houghton, 1888.
A Daughter of Eve. Boston, Ticknor, 1889.
Story of Lawrence Garthe. Boston and New York, Houghton, 1894.
LEE, MARGARET
Lorimer and Wife. Harlan, 1881.
Divorce. Lovell, 1882.
A Brighton Night. Lovell, 1885.
Dr. Wilmer's Love. Lovell, 1886.
Lizzie Adriance. Munro, 1889.
A Brooklyn Bachelor. Lovell, 1890.
One Touch of Nature. Taylor, 1892.
LIPPARD, GEORGE
The Quaker City; or, The Monks of Monk Hall. A Romance of Philadelphia Life, Mystery and Crime. Phila., published by the author, 1847. First edition, 1844.
The Bank Director's Son. A Real and Intensely Interesting Revelation of City Life. Phila., Barclay and Orton, 1851.
The Nazarene; or, The Last of the Washingtons. A Revelation of Philadelphia, New York and Washington in the year 1844. Phila., Peterson, 1854. First edition, 1846.

The Empire City; or, New York by Night and Day. Its Aristocracy and Its Dollars. Phila., Peterson, 1864. First edition, 1853.

LONGSTREET, MRS. ABBY BUCHANAN (Rachel Buchanan)
A Debutante in New York Society. Appleton, 1888.

McCLELLAN, MRS. GEORGE (Harford Fleming, pseud.)
A Carpet Knight. Boston and New York, Houghton, 1885.

MATTHEWS, JAMES BRANDER
His Father's Son. Harper, 1895.
A Confident To-Morrow. New York and London, Harper, 1900.
The Action and the Word. New York and London, Harper, 1900.

MATTHEWS, JAMES BRANDER and JESSOP, GEORGE H.
Check and Counter-Check. Lippincott's Magazine, Jan., 1888. Published in book form as *A Tale of 25 Hours.* Appleton, 1892.

MILLER, JOAQUIN
The Destruction of Gotham. New York and London, Funk and Wagnalls, 1886.

MITCHELL, DR. SILAS WEIR
In War Time. Boston, Houghton, 1885. (Atlantic Monthly, Jan., 1884, to Dec., 1884).
Roland Blake. Boston, Houghton, 1886.
Characteristics. Century, 1892.

MOORE, JOHN M.
The Adventures of Tom Stapleton. Garrett, 185-. (Brother Jonathan, Jan. 1, 1842, to May 14, 1842).

MORFORD, HENRY
Shoulder Straps. A Novel of New York and the Army. 1862. Phila., Peterson, 1863.
The Days of Shoddy. A Novel of the Great Rebellion in 1861. Phila., Peterson. (1863.)
The Coward. A Novel of Society and the Field in 1863. Phila., Peterson. (1864.)

MOWATT, MRS. ANNA CORA—See under Mrs. Ritchie.

MYERS, P. HAMILTON
The Miser's Heir. Phila., Peterson, 1854.
Roxy Hastings; or, A Raffle for Life. Street and Smith, 1890.

NEAL, JOHN
Randolph. 2 v. (Baltimore) 1823.
True Womanhood. Boston, Ticknor, 1859.

NEWELL, ROBERT H. (Orpheus C. Kerr, pseud.)
Avery Glibun; or, Between Two Fires. Carleton, 1867.
The Walking Doll; or, The Asters and Disasters of Society. Felt, 1871.

OTIS, MRS. HARRISON GRAY
The Barclays of Boston. Boston, Ticknor, 1854.

PHELPS, MRS. ELIZABETH (Stuart)
A Peep at "Number Five"; or, A Chapter in the Life of a City Pastor. Boston, Phillips, Sampson, 1852.

POOL, MARIA LOUISE
Roweny in Boston. Harper, 1892.
Mrs. Keats Bradford. Harper, 1892.

RAHM, IDA
Miss Nancy. Phila., McKay, 1884.

RIDEING, WILLIAM H.
A Little Upstart. Boston, Cupples, Upham, 1885.

RITCHIE, MRS. ANNA CORA MOWATT (Helen Berkley, pseud.)
The Fortune Hunter. A Novel of New York Society. Phila., 1842.

ROE, EDWARD P.
What Can She Do? Edinburgh: Edmonston and Douglas, 1874. First edition, 1873.
Without a Home. Dodd, Mead, 1881.
An Original Belle. Dodd, Mead, 1885.

ROWSON, MRS. SUSANNA H.
Charlotte Temple. Phila., M. Carey, 1794. Reprint of this edition was published by Funk and Wagnalls, New York and London, 1905.

RUSH, REBECCA
Kelroy. By a Lady of Pennsylvania. Phila. and New York, Bradford and Inskeep, 1812.

SALTUS, EDGAR E.
Eden. An Episode. Chicago, Belford, Clarke, 1888.
A Transaction in Hearts. Lippincott's Magazine, Feb. 1889.

SAVAGE, RICHARD H.
Delilah of Harlem. A Story of the New York City of To-Day. American News Co., 1893.
A Daughter of Judas—a fin-de-siécle tale of New York city life. Chicago and New York, Neely, 1894.
Checked Through. Missing Trunk No. 17580. Chicago and New York, Rand, McNally, 1896.
An Exile from London. Home Pub. Co., 1896.
In the Swim—a Story of Currents and Undercurrents in Gayest New York. Chicago and New York, Rand McNally, 1898.

SCHEMIL, PETER (pseud.)
Lights and Shadows of Fashionable Life. Knickerbocker Magazine, Feb., 1846, to August, 1846.

SEARING, MRS. ANNIE ELIZA (Pidgeon)
A Social Experiment. New York and London, Putnam, 1885.

SEATON, WALTER
A Man in Search of a Wife; or, the Adventures of a Bachelor in New York. De Witt, 1853.

SEDGWICK, CATHERINE MARIA
Clarence; or, a Tale of Our Own Times. Revised edition, Putnam, 1849. First edition, 1830.
Married or Single. 2 v. Harper, 1857.

SHERWOOD, MRS. MARY E.
A Transplanted Rose: a Story of New York Society. Harper, 1882.
Sweet Brier. Boston, Lothrop, 1889.

SMITH, F. HOPKINSON
Colonel Carter of Cartersville. Boston and New York, Houghton, 1892.

STEPHENS, MRS. ANNE S.
High Life in New York. By Jonathan Slick, Esq. 2 v. London, 1844.

STIMSON, FREDERIC J.(J. S. of Dale, pseud.)
The Crime of Henry Vane. Scribner, 1884.
First Harvests. Scribner, 1888.

STOCKTON, FRANK R.
The Hundredth Man. Century, 1887.

STOWE, MRS. HARRIET BEECHER
MY Wife and I. Boston and New York, Houghton, 1871.
We and Our Neighbors. Boston and New York, Houghton, 1873.

SULLIVAN, THOMAS R.
Roses of Shadow. Scribner, 1885.

TAYLOR, BAYARD
John Godfrey's Fortunes. Putnam, 1865.

THOMAS, FREDERICK W.
Clinton Bradshaw. 2 v. Phila., Carey, Lea and Blanchard, 1835.
East and West. 2 v. Phila., Carey, Lea and Blanchard, 1836.
Howard Pinckney. Phila., Lea and Blanchard, 1840.

THOMPSON, JULIA C.
Life in Narrow Streets. Phila., Presbyterian Board of Publication,
1871.

TOWNSEND, EDWARD W.
A Daughter of the Tenements. Lovell, Coryell, 1895.

TRASK, MRS. KATE (Katrina Trask)
White Satin and Homespun. Anson, Randolph, 1896.
John Leighton, Jr. Harper, 1898.

TRUMBULL, ANNIE ELIOT
A Cape Cod Week. Barnes, 1898.

WARNER, CHARLES DUDLEY
A Little Journey in the World. New York and London, Harper, 1889.
The Golden House. Harper, 1895.
That Fortune. New York and London, Harper, 1899.
The Gilded Age. (With Samuel L. Clements). 2 v. Harper, 1873.

WARNER, SUSAN (Elizabeth Wetherell, pseud.)
The Wide Wide World. Putnam, 1850.

WELLS, KATE G. (Mrs. Catherine B. Wells)
Miss Curtis. Boston, Ticknor, 1888.

WHITE, ELIZA ORNE
Miss Brooks. Boston, Roberts, 1890.

WILLET, W. N.
Charles Vincent; or, The Two Clerks. A Tale of Commercial Life.
3 v. Harper, 1839.

WILLIAMS, HENRY L., JR.
The Steel Safe; or, The Stains and Splendors of New York Life.
De Witt, 1868.

WILLIS, N. P.
Paul Fane; or, Parts of a Life Else Untold. Scribner, 1857.

WINTER, MRS. AND BOY, MRS. (Griswold, Jane Emmett, pseud.)
The Lost Wedding Ring. Putnam, 1887.

WINTHROP, THEODORE
Ceceil Dreme. Lovell, 1862.

WOOD, CHARLOTTE D. (Charlotte Dunning, pseud.)
A Step Aside. Boston, Houghton, 1886.

WOOD, JOHN SEYMOUR
Gramercy Park. A Story of New York. Appleton, 1892.

YARDLEY, MRS. JANE (Woolsey)
A Superior Woman. Boston, Roberts, 1885.

INDEX